Readings
in
Economics

Readings
in
Economics

Second Edition • 1981

AMERICAN INSTITUTE FOR
PROPERTY AND LIABILITY UNDERWRITERS
Providence and Sugartown Roads, Malvern, Pennsylvania 19355

ACKNOWLEDGMENTS

Reading 1 is reproduced from the following work with the permission of the publisher. Campbell R. McConnell, *Economics*, 8th Edition, McGraw-Hill Book Company, © 1981 by McGraw-Hill, Inc.

Readings 2 and 11 are reproduced from the following works with the permission of the publisher. Gregory Schmid, "Productivity and Re-industrialization: A Dissenting View," and Lyle E. Gramley, "The Role of Supply-Side Economics in Fighting Inflation," *Challenge*, Jan/Feb 1981 © 1981 by M. E. Sharpe, Inc.

Reading 3 is reproduced from the following work with the permission of the publisher. Richard B. McKenzie and Gordon Tullock, *The New World of Economics*, 3rd Edition, © 1981 by Richard D. Irwin, Inc.

Readings 4, 5, 6, 7, 8, and 9 are reproduced from the following work with the permission of the publisher. Lawrence S. Ritter and William L. Silber, *Money*, Fourth and Revised Edition, Basic Books, Inc., © 1981 by Lawrence S. Ritter and William L. Silber.

Readings 10, 12, and 14 are reproduced from the following work with the permission of the publisher. Richard H. Leftwich and Ansel M. Sharp, *Economics of Social Issues*, 4th Edition, © 1980 by Business Publications, Inc.

Reading 13 is reproduced from *The Economic Report of the President —January 1980* and *January 1981*, United States Government Printing Office.

Foreword

The American Institute for Property and Liability Underwriters and the Insurance Institute of America are companion, nonprofit, educational organizations supported by the property-liability insurance industry. Their purpose is to provide quality continuing education programs for insurance personnel.

The Insurance Institute of America offers programs leading to the Certificate in General Insurance, the Associate in Claims (AIC) designation, the Associate in Management (AIM) designation, the Associate in Risk Management (ARM) designation, the Associate in Underwriting (AIU) designation, the Associate in Loss Control Management (ALCM) designation, the Associate in Premium Auditing (APA) designation, and the Accredited Adviser in Insurance (AAI) designation. The American Institute develops, maintains, and administers the educational program leading to the Chartered Property Casualty Underwriter (CPCU) professional designation.

Throughout the history of the CPCU program an annual updating of parts of the course of study took place. But as changes in the insurance industry came about at an increasingly rapid pace, and as the world in which insurance operates grew increasingly complex, it became clear that a thorough, fundamental revision of the CPCU curriculum was necessary. This text is one of those which were developed specifically for, and published by, the American Institute for use in the revised 10-semester CPCU curriculum which was introduced in 1978.

Throughout the development of the CPCU text series, it was—and will continue to be—necessary to draw on the knowledge and skills of Institute staff members. These individuals will receive no royalties on texts sold and their writing responsibilities are seen as an integral part of their professional duties. We have proceeded in this way to avoid any possibility of conflicts of interests. All Institute textbooks have been—and will continue to be—subjected to an extensive review process. Reviewers are drawn from both industry and academic ranks.

We welcome criticisms of our publications. Such comments should be directed to the Curriculum department of the Institutes.

Edwin S. Overman, Ph.D., CPCU
President

v

Table of Contents

READING 1

Tenets of Capitalism

Strictly speaking, pure capitalism has never existed and probably never will. Why, then, do we bother to consider the operation of such an economy? Because it gives us a very rough *first approximation* of how modern American capitalism functions. And approximations or models, when properly handled, can be very useful. In other words, pure capitalism constitutes a simplified model which we shall then modify and adjust to correspond more closely to the reality of American capitalism.

Unfortunately, there is no neat and universally accepted definition of capitalism. We are therefore required to examine in some detail the basic tenets of capitalism to acquire a comprehensive understanding of what pure capitalism entails. In short, the framework of capitalism embodies the following institutions and assumptions: (1) private property, (2) freedom of enterprise and choice, (3) self-interest as the dominant motive, (4) competition, (5) reliance upon the price system, and (6) a limited role for government.

Private Property

Under a capitalistic system, property resources are owned by private individuals and private institutions rather than by government. Private property, coupled with the freedom to negotiate binding legal contracts, permits private persons or businesses to obtain, control, employ, and dispose of economic resources as they see fit. The

1

institution of private property is sustained over time by the *right to bequeath*, that is, by the right of a property owner to designate the recipient of this property at the time of death.

Needless to say, there are broad legal limits to this right of private ownership. For example, the use of one's resources for the production of narcotics is prohibited by law. Nor is public ownership nonexistent. Even in pure capitalism, recognition is given to the fact that public ownership of certain "natural monopolies" may be essential to the achievement of efficiency in the use of resources.

Freedom of Enterprise and Choice

Closely related to private ownership of property is freedom of enterprise and choice. Capitalism charges its component economic units with the responsibility of making certain choices, which are registered and made effective through the free markets of the economy.

Freedom of enterprise means that under pure capitalism, private business enterprises are free to obtain economic resources, to organize these resources in the production of a good or service of the firm's own choosing, and to sell it in the markets of their choice. No artificial obstacles or restrictions imposed by government or other producers block an entrepreneur's choice to enter or leave a particular industry.

Freedom of choice means that owners of property resources and money capital can employ or dispose of these resources as they see fit. It also means that laborers are free to enter any of those lines of work for which they are qualified. Finally, it means that consumers are at liberty, within the limits of their money incomes, to buy that collection of goods and services which they feel is most appropriate in satisfying their wants. Freedom of consumer choice may well be the most profound of these freedoms. The consumer is in a particularly strategic position in a capitalistic economy; in a sense, the consumer is sovereign. The range of free choices for suppliers of human and property resources is circumscribed by the choices of consumers. The consumer ultimately decides what the capitalistic economy should produce, and resource suppliers must make their free choices within the boundaries thereby delineated. Resource suppliers and businesses are not really "free" to produce goods and services consumers do not desire.

Again, broad legal limitations prevail in the expression of all these free choices.

Role of Self-Interest

Since capitalism is an individualistic system, it is not surprising to find that the primary driving force of such an economy is the promotion of one's self-interest; each economic unit attempts to do what is best for itself. Hence, entrepreneurs aim at the maximization of their firms' profits or, as the case might be, the minimization of losses. And, other things being equal, owners of property resources attempt to achieve the highest price obtainable from the rent or sale of these resources. Given the amount and irksomeness of the effort involved, those who supply human resources will also attempt to obtain the highest possible incomes from their employment. Consumers, in purchasing a given product, will seek to obtain it at the lowest price. In short, capitalism presumes self-interest as the fundamental *modus operandi* for the various economic units as they express their free choices. The motive of self-interest gives direction and consistency to what might otherwise be an extremely chaotic economy.

Although self-interest is the basic motive underlying the functioning of capitalism, there are exceptions to the rule: Businesses and individuals do not always act in their own self-interest. Altruistic motives are part of the makeup of economic units. Yet, self-interest is the best single statement of how economic units actually behave.

Competition

Freedom of choice exercised in terms of promoting one's own monetary returns provides the basis for competition, or economic rivalry, as a fundamental feature of capitalism. Competition, as economists see it, entails:

1 The presence of large numbers of independently acting buyers and sellers operating in the market for any particular product or resource.

2 The freedom of buyers and sellers to enter or leave particular markets.

Let us briefly explore these two related aspects of competition:

Large Numbers The essence of competition is the widespread diffusion of economic power within the two major aggregates— businesses and households—which comprise the economy. When a large number of buyers and sellers are present in a particular market, no one buyer or seller will be able to demand or offer a quantity of the product sufficiently large to noticeably influence its price. Let us examine this statement in terms of the selling or supply side of the product market.

We have all observed that when a product becomes unusually scarce, its price will rise. For example, an unseasonable frost in Florida may seriously curtail the output of citrus crops and sharply increase the price of orange juice. Similarly, *if* a single producer, or a small group of producers acting together, can somehow control or restrict the total supply of a product, then price can be raised to the seller's advantage. By controlling supply, the producer can "rig the market" on his or her own behalf. Now the essence of competition is that there are so many sellers that each, *because he or she is contributing an almost negligible fraction of the total supply*, has virtually no control over the supply or, therefore, over the product price.

For example, suppose there are 10,000 farmers, each of whom is supplying 100 bushels of corn in the Kansas City grain market at some particular time when the price of corn happens to be $4 per bushel. Could a single farmer who feels dissatisfied with the existing price cause an artificial scarcity of corn and thereby boost the price above $4? The answer is obviously "No." Farmer Jones, by restricting output from 100 to 75 bushels, exerts virtually no effect upon the total supply of corn. In fact, total supply is reduced only from 1,000,000 to 999,975 bushels. This obviously is not much of a shortage! Supply is virtually unchanged, and, therefore, the $4 price persists. In brief, competition means that each seller is providing a drop in the bucket of total supply. Individual sellers can make no noticeable dent in total supply; hence, a seller cannot *as an individual producer*[1] manipulate product price. This is what is meant when it is pointed out that an individual competitive seller is "at the mercy of the market."

The same rationale applies to the demand side of the market. Buyers are plentiful and act independently. Thus single buyers cannot manipulate the market to their advantage.

The important point is this: *The widespread diffusion of economic power underlying competition controls the use and limits the potential abuse of that power*. Economic rivalry prevents economic units from wreaking havoc upon one another as they attempt to further their self-interests. Competition imposes limits upon expressions of self-interest by buyers and sellers. Competition is a basic regulatory force in capitalism.

---

[1] Of course, if a number of farmers simultaneously restricted their production, the resulting change in total supply could no longer be ignored, and price would rise. Competition (a large number of sellers) implies the impossibility of such collusion.

Entry and Exit   Competition also assumes that it is a simple matter for producers to enter (or leave) a particular industry; there are no artificial legal or institutional obstacles to prohibit the expansion (or contraction) of specific industries. This aspect of competition is prerequisite to the flexibility which is essential if an economy is to remain efficient over time. Freedom of entry is necessary if the economy is to adjust appropriately to changes in consumer tastes, technology, or resource supplies.

Markets and Prices

The basic coordinating mechanism of a capitalist economy is the market or price system. *Capitalism is a market economy.* The decisions rendered by the buyers and sellers of products and resources are made effective through a system of markets. The preferences of sellers and buyers are registered on the supply and demand sides of various markets, and the outcome of these choices is a system of product and resource prices. These prices are guideposts upon which resource owners, entrepreneurs, and consumers make and revise their free choices in furthering their self-interests. Just as competition is the controlling mechanism, so a system of markets and prices is a basic organizing force. The price system is an elaborate communication system through which innumerable individual free choices are recorded, summarized, and balanced against one another. Those who obey the dictates of the price system are rewarded; those who ignore them are penalized by the system. Through this communication system, society renders its decisions concerning what the economy should produce, how production can be efficiently organized, and how the fruits of productive endeavor are to be distributed among the individual economic units which make up capitalism.

Not only is the price system the mechanism through which society renders decisions concerning how it allocates its resources and distributes the resulting output, but it is through the price system that these decisions are carried out. However, a word of caution: Economic systems based upon the ideologies of socialism and communism also depend upon price systems, but not to the same degree or in the same way as does pure capitalism. Socialistic and communistic societies use markets and prices primarily to implement the decisions made wholly or in part by a central planning authority. In capitalism, the price system functions both as a device for registering innumerable choices of free individuals and businesses *and* as a mechanism for carrying out these decisions.

Limited Government

A competitive capitalist economy is thought to be conducive to a high degree of efficiency in the use or allocation of its resources. Hence, there is allegedly little real need for governmental intervention in the operation of such an economy beyond its aforementioned role of imposing broad legal limits upon the exercise of individual choices and the use of private property. The concept of pure capitalism as a self-regulating and self-adjusting type of economy precludes any significant economic role for government. Capitalism in practice has not been self-regulating to the degree economists once supposed, and governments play a significant role in present-day mixed capitalism.

READING 2

Productivity and Reindustrialization: A Dissenting View

Falling rates of productivity growth have been singled out as the critical U.S. economic failing of recent years. Presidential commissions, official government publications, the academic community, and business journalists have all focused attention on this issue. The fall in the growth rate of productivity has become a yardstick of everything fundamentally wrong with the U.S. economy, from a decline in international competitiveness to a failure in the American educational system to a loss of the will to work. It has stimulated a whole industry of policy analysts and politicians asserting the need for "reindustrialization" or "revitalization."

The focus on productivity, however, is actually a fundamental misinterpretation of recent economic history, and the policy prescriptions it is generating could pose a genuine threat to long-term U.S. economic growth. The fall in productivity growth rates during the 1970s was a direct consequence of revolutionary increase in the U.S. labor force which made labor cheap relative to capital. The consequent substitution of skilled labor for capital did not affect long-term growth prospects: the buildup of the U.S. capital stock continued and, if anything, the basic competitiveness of U.S. products in the international markets improved. In fact, the response to the major changes in the labor markets in the last fifteen years reflects one of the prime American virtues: the vigorous adaptability of the U.S. economy.

Declining Productivity

Productivity is a measure of the relationship between the amount of goods and services produced and all the inputs used in the production

7

of that output. The measure is most useful if output can be stated in terms of the variation in a single input. While any number of input measures can be used, including land, resources, and capital, the most commonly used measure, and the one we will concentrate on, is that associated with labor: output per hour of all persons employed.

There is no serious debate over the fact that there was a decline in productivity growth in the United States in the 1970s. Between 1948 and 1965, output per hour of all persons in the private sector rose an average of 3.2 percent per year; between 1965 and 1973, it rose an average of 2.3 percent per year; between 1974 and 1979, 0.6 percent per year. Most other measures of labor productivity show a similar decline over that period.

Even from a long-term perspective, the decline in productivity growth in recent years stands out. From 1874 to 1973, productivity growth in the United States averaged 2.3 percent per year. Except for the first years of the Great Depression (1929-1934), there has not been an extended period of such low productivity growth rate since the era of mass immigration before World War I. It seems reasonable to conclude that the decline in the rate of productivity is real—and significant.

The Labor Market Revolution

The focus on aggregate productivity statistics masks the complex structural adjustments among key component elements. The most important structural change in recent years has been the virtual revolution in the U.S. labor market. The U.S. economy has absorbed a huge number of labor force entrants over the last fifteen years. The entrants came from two sources: the maturing of the postwar baby boom generation and the movement of women into the labor force.

The postwar baby boom broke a long pattern of declining fertility rates in the United States. Between 1925 and 1945, total fertility rates (or the number of births each woman would have in her lifetime if current birthrates for each age group remained unchanged) averaged 2.5; between 1945 and 1965, they averaged 3.4 (with a high of 3.8 in 1965); since 1965, they have averaged 2.2 (with a current low of 1.8). This baby boom produced an abnormally large population cohort which began to have an appreciable effect on the labor force in the mid-1960s (Figure 2-1).

Coincident with the maturing of the baby-boom generation, an increasing portion of the female population chose to enter and remain in the labor force. While women's participation rates have been rising

Figure 2-1   **Population and Labor Force**
*(percent change in total population and
total labor force)*

Source: *Current Population Reports*, Series P-23.

steadily since the late 1940s, the rate of increase in participation has soared since the mid-1960s (Table 2-1).

A third aspect of the revolution was the jump in the level of education of young labor force entrants. The number of young people who went to college and graduate school mushroomed during the 1960s and early 1970s (Table 2-2).

In sum, starting in the mid-1960s, the U.S. economy absorbed a startling number of relatively well-educated young people and older women. In the 17 years from 1948 to 1965, the labor force expanded by

Table 2-1   **Female Participation Rates, 1948-1979**

	Percent of female population 16 and over in labor force		Annual average percent increase
1948	32.7		
		1948-65	1.1
1965	39.3		
		1966-79	1.9
1979	51.0		

Table 2-2 **Degrees Earned**
(in thousands)

Type of degree	1950	1960	1975
B.A.	432.1	392.4	922.9
Post-Graduate	64.6	110.8	382.5

Source: Digest of Education Statistics, 1979, p. 123.

13.8 million or an average of 811,000 per year; in the 14 years from 1966 to 1979, it expanded by 28.5 million, or an average of 2,035,000 per year. To put it another way, while the labor force as a percentage of total population actually fell between 1948 and 1965, it has risen since, especially in the mid- and late-1970s as young people flocked into the labor force and had fewer children of their own (Table 2-3).

The impact of the growth in the number of young, well-educated people on the economy was mitigated for a time by the temporary increase in the size of the armed forces. By the early 1970s, this effect began to disappear: between 1970 and 1975, the total number of people in the armed forces fell by one million. By all measures, the growth in the civilian labor force was higher after 1973.

The major impact of this growth in the labor force was a fall in the cost of labor relative to other inputs. The average hourly earnings of workers in the private nonagricultural sector, when adjusted for inflation, rose at an annual rate of 2.5 percent from 1948 through 1965; rose 1.6 percent per year from 1966 through 1973; and actually fell by 0.6

Table 2-3 **Employment per Capita, 1948-1979**

	Civilian labor force as a percent of total civilian population		Annual average percent increase
1948	41.8		
		1948-65	−0.4
1965	38.9		
		1966-73	1.1
1973	42.6		
		1974-79	1.7
1979	47.1		

Figure 2-2   Relative Cost of Capital and Labor

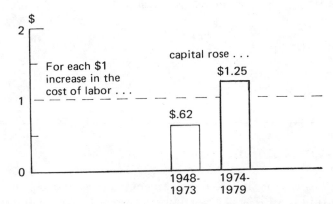

Source: *Economic Report of the President*, 1980, pp. 244, 265.

percent per year from 1974 to 1979. In the meantime, businessmen found that the cost of capital goods—plant, equipment, and structure—relative to labor was rising sharply (Figure 2-2). With the relative cost of labor becoming lower, it was reasonable for entrepreneurs to invest in processes that tended to use more skilled labor at the expense of increasingly costly capital equipment. The fall in productivity was a direct reflection of this substitution of relatively cheap labor for expensive capital equipment.

Productivity and Growth

A direct causal connection between productivity and growth is difficult to make. The shift toward a more labor-intensive economy did coincide with a decline in real GNP growth rates (Table 2-4), though the decline in GNP growth was much smaller than the decline in productivity. But many special factors that affected demand between 1973 and 1979 could account for the decline in GNP: the large shift in the relative costs of energy, the severity of the world recession in 1974-75, the overall slowdown in growth rates of the European consumer economies, and the growth in government regulations.

Theoretically, the structural change that favored labor relative to capital could hurt long-term economic prospects in one of two ways: the emphasis on relatively cheap labor could retard the necessary buildup in the U.S. capital stock, or it could affect the relative competitiveness of U.S. industries in the world environment.

Table 2-4   Productivity and GNP

	Productivity	Real GNP
1948-65	3.2	3.8
1966-73	2.3	3.7
1974-79	0.6	2.5

Capital Investment

The rate of growth in real investment per worker declined dramatically during the 1970s as the number of workers grew rapidly (Table 2-5). But investment as a percentage of GNP fell only slightly during the mid- and late 1970s and, in fact, was higher in the late 1970s than in the period 1948-65. In addition, the growth in the real net stock of business capital was as high during the mid- and late 1970s as it was during the 1950s and early 1960s, though it was lower than it had been during the boom years of the late 1960s. Given the fact that the relative cost of capital rose dramatically during the 1970s, the basic stability of real investment is impressive. On the whole, private sector investment has held up well despite a major increase in relative costs of capital, and the growth in the capital stock during the 1970s seems consistent with longer-term trends.

International Competitiveness

The second signal of a potential problem would be a decline in world competitiveness of U.S. products. Other countries, both devel-

Table 2-5   Real Investment, 1948-1979

	Percent increase in real investment per worker	Real investment as percent of real GNP
1948-65	2.5	9.2
1966-73	1.8	10.3
1974-79	−0.4	9.9

Source: Economic Report of the President, 1980, pp. 204, 303.

oped and developing, have had much higher rates of productivity growth than the United States since the early 1950s. But this does not mean that they have become more productive than the United States. Rather, they are growing faster because they are still catching up with this country. The European countries and Japan fell well behind U.S. levels of output per worker hour during the two world wars and the Great Depression. Their postwar productivity growth spurts have now brought the overall productivity rates of other major industrial countries up to about 75 percent of the average U.S level of productivity. Japan averages slightly below 55 percent of the average U.S. level. Since adapting selected technology from a high-productivity country is easier than improving productivity where there is no more advanced model to draw on, it is not surprising that other countries have higher gains than the United States does.

The same holds true if comparisons are made in specific categories of products that are technology-intensive. The United States has long had an international advantage in technologically intensive, high value-added products. A change in the relative competitiveness of these products due to inadequate labor productivity is likely to be felt quickly in the international markets. A recent Department of Labor study examined the long-term international market performance of the 17 most technology-intensive industries. Technology-intensive industries were defined as those industries at the three-digit Standard International Trade Classification (SITC) level which had the highest expenditures for research and development per unit of output. The net exports (total exports minus total imports) for those 17 industries were compared for three time periods: 1962, 1970, and 1977 (Table 2-6). Net exports reflect the best single measure of a country's trade performance relative to the world and between commodities. Table 2-6 shows that these technological-intensive industries increased their export surplus during the 1970s after losing ground during the 1960s. Preliminary data indicate that the trend toward surplus on these 17 items continued in the late 1970s, rising from $5.8 billion in 1977 to $10.2 billion in 1979. The performance of high-technology industries was thus substantially better during the 1970s than it had been in the 1960s. In fact, the table probably understates the true competitiveness of U.S. high-technology industries. It is based upon three-digit SITC categories that are aggregations of a sometimes diverse group of components. For example, SITC category 724, telecommunications apparatus, includes TV sets, radio receivers, and telephone and telecommunications equipment. If the trade data are disaggregated, virtually all of the increase in deficit is accounted for by a rise in net imports of relatively low value-added per worker TV and radio equipment. (Radio and TV receivers averaged a value-added of $13.65 per person-hour worked,

Table 2-6

U.S. Technology-Intensive Manufactured Goods, 1962-1977

SITC	Description	1962	Net exports (millions of current U.S. $) 1970	1977
724	Telecommunication apparatus	226.4	−442.2	−1,624.3
714	Office machines	242.8	1,042.0	2,055.4
734	Aircraft	1,155.3	2,382.2	5,261.5
541	Medicinal and pharmaceutical products	220.1	333.1	761.1
726	Electrical apparatus for medical purposes	4.3	19.3	116.7
711	Power generating machinery	371.5	622.7	1,372.5
514	Other inorganic chemicals	−14.4	77.6	257.3
864	Watches and clocks	−68.8	−163.3	−538.1
513	Inorganic chemicals	53.4	−21.4	−386.2
862	Photographic supplies	41.8	152.2	521.4
861	Scientific, medical controlling instruments	213.1	500.5	911.4
571	Explosives and pyrotechnics	7.2	−7.4	43.3
581	Plastic materials	289.5	530.0	1,332.0
722	Electric power machinery	230.1	364.0	1,327.0
725	Domestic electrical equipment	89.3	−23.9	−21.9
723	Equipment for distributing electricity	35.1	−53.6	182.6
732	Road motor vehicles	754.4	−1,930.6	−5,732.9
	Net exports of technology-intensive goods	3,851.1	3,381.2	5,838.8

while other telecommunications equipment averaged $17.00.) Subtracting trade in radio and TV sets, category 724 shows a surplus of $274.3 million in 1970 and $119.6 million in 1977.

Similarly, the growth in the surplus in office machines (SITC 714) was held back by a growing deficit in relatively low value-added typewriters and electric-mechanical calculating machines. (Value-added in these categories averages $12.18 per person-hour as opposed to $26.78 in computer equipment.) If these two categories are removed, the surplus of other office equipment, including computers and duplicating machines, rose from $728.1 million in 1970 to $2,523.8 million in 1977. Eliminating the low value-added per worker subcategories of radio and TV receivers, typewriters, and desk calculators, the overall export surplus of technology-intensive industries jumps from $3,783.8 million in 1970 to $8,051.1 million in 1977.

Further, in two marginal categories of consumer goods—autos and domestic appliances—both R&D expenditures and value-added per worker are only slightly above the overall industry average. Eliminating these two categories from the list of 17 would further boost the positive balance to $5,414.4 million in 1970 and $13,784.0 million in 1977. In other words, during the 1970s the United States did remarkably well in competition with the rest of the world in the most technology-intensive products, and its performance seems to improve as the technological sophistication of the product increases. In those products which depend less on R&D and have a lower value-added per worker, foreign competitors have been increasing their penetration of the U.S. market. Thus, the fall in the relative price of skilled labor and the rise in the relative price of capital during the 1970s and the consequent substitution of labor for capital does not seem to have affected the long-term comparative advantage of the United States. This country has continued to increase its export surplus in technology-intensive goods and has continued to lose net market position in goods that have much lower levels of value-added per employee.

On balance, the use of more labor in the economy and the subsequent fall in the growth rate of output per worker during the last 15 years has not affected long-term growth prospects: the share of GNP being invested has remained the same, and the competitiveness of U.S. high-technology products in the international markets has, if anything, improved.

The 1980s

The 1980s will witness important changes in the labor force. By mid-decade, the baby-boom cohort will be almost fully absorbed, and the rate of increase in women's participation rates is likely to slow as their rates approach men's at certain age levels. The annual growth in the labor force is likely to fall to one-third of its earlier peak level by the late 1980s (Table 2-7). As the rate of increase in the labor force declines, the relative cost of labor should rise. The opportunities to substitute relatively cheaper capital for labor should grow (that is, more robots will be used on assembly lines, and more sophisticated word-processing machines in offices). By the mid-1980s, fundamental market forces should help to stimulate capital investment and raise the level of output per worker. In all likelihood, the productivity growth rate will return to its secular average of 2 or 2.5 percent. From a longer-term perspective, the fall in productivity rates during the 1970s will be seen as a rational market response to the unique labor market factors of the time, a response that did not interfere with the two critical elements of U.S. long-term growth: the accumulation of capital stock and the international comparative advantage in technology-intensive goods.

Policy Implications

The fall in productivity growth rates has spurred discussion of a number of government programs for reindustrialization to foster "productive" capital investment and R&D expenditures. Congress has held hearings and discussions on bills that would:
   accelerate depreciation schedules
- lower the capital-gains tax
- raise the level of the investment tax credit
- reduce the burden of government regulations.
Each of these policy steps has costs. In many of them, government revenues would be cut substantially, and either taxes would have to be raised, other government programs cut back, or an inflationary

Table 2-7	Total Labor Force
	(average rate of increase)
1965-70	2.2
1971-75	2.0
1976-80	2.6
1981-85	1.6
1986-90	0.9

government deficit financed. No consensus exists for a reduction in government health, safety, and environmental regulations. The benefits in terms of increased incentives to invest might be substantial, but their prime beneficiaries would likely be capital-intensive, high-technology companies that are doing just fine without them. If the intention of the reindustrialization programs is to aid those industries that are bearing the brunt of foreign competition, then they can be targeted much more clearly through outright protectionist measures. But do we need to keep employees tied to jobs in noncompetitive, low value-added industries just as we enter a period of potential labor shortages? The actual impact of the reindustrialization programs could be to reduce flexibility that has characterized America's response to changing circumstances.

The United States faces many serious problems in the 1980s: trade adjustment, inflation, energy and resource availability, education and training of urban youth. A major program of reindustrialization to improve productivity? Let relative wages rise and forget about it.

READING 3

The Laffer (not laughter) Curve

For several decades, the name of John Maynard Keynes was treated with considerable reverence in economic literature. He was the British economist who, back in the 1930s, literally revolutionized the way most economists and government policymakers thought about the function and importance of government fiscal (i.e., tax and expenditure) policy. Before Keynes, economists tended to argue that any unemployment or sluggishness in the economy will be eliminated by "natural" movements in market prices and wages. If there are more people seeking jobs than there are jobs available, then through competitive forces, wages will fall; the number of jobs will expand; the number of people looking for work will contract; and eventually the market will clear. Unemployment that persists for a long period of time can be attributed to "obstructions" in the market, such as minimum-wage laws and union contracts, that prevent the wage rate from falling.

After Keynes, economists—following the lead of Keynes—argued that unemployment can persist "naturally" in free, uncontrolled markets of consumers and investors. The cause of the persistent unemployment, insufficient (aggregate) demand. The so-called Keynesian economists reasoned that the demand of consumers for goods and services is determined by, among other things, the income level; the higher the income, the greater the consumption demand and vice versa. Investment, on the other hand, is determined by a number of factors, such as expected profits on plant and equipment and the interest rate on borrowed funds. Since savers and investors were different groups of people and since (or so it was believed) interest rates do not necessarily adjust downward when savings (at a given income level) exceed investments, the total demand of consumers and investors may at times not be sufficient to buy the total output of the economy. Hence, realizing that their inventories are

19

piling up (when goods that were produced are left unsold), businesses will cut back on production, incomes will fall, and unemployment will arise. In short, Keynesians argued that at the full-employment income level, the total demand in the economy may fall short of total production and unemployment can then emerge and can persist. Again, the cause of persistent unemployment, insufficient demand.

Before Keynes, most economists tended to believe that aside from removing obstrucions to downward wage movements, the government has no role to play in alleviating unemployment. After Keynes, most economists came to believe that government has a very important function in the macroeconomy: the stimulation of aggregate demand through its own purchases and through cuts in its tax collection. If unemployment is caused by insufficient aggregate demand, then it can be alleviated by greater government demand and/or by greater consumer demand that is induced by cuts in the taxes people pay.

Before Keynes, most economists equated deficits in government budgets with "irresponsible" government spending. After Keynes, budget deficits were seen and promoted as a means of increasing aggregate demand, thereby, as a means of stimulating an expansion in the national income level and reducing persistent unemployment. (A deficit in the government's budget means the government is spending more than it is collecting in taxes. Therefore, the government contributes more to total demand in terms of its own expenditures than it subtracts from total demand through the taxes it collects.)

During the 1950s, the federal government frequently ran budgetary deficits. However, the deficits were never (openly) advocated as a means of stimulating the domestic economy. The Eisenhower administration was always defensive about its deficits, blaming them on Congress. Congress, in turn, blamed the deficits on each other and the administration. President John Kennedy openly adopted Keynesian fiscal remedies for unemployment and retarded growth in national income. In the 1960s and through the early years of the 1970s, much of the professional attention of economists was directed at finding means of expanding, in the most effective way, total demand in the economy. In 1962 Kennedy proposed a tax reduction of about $10 billion (or 10 percent of total tax collections at that time) and suggested that the resulting budgetary deficit was "good" for the economy; it would get the "economy moving again" through its effect on demand.

Throughout the late 1960s there was a small band of economists at schools like the University of Chicago (called *monetarists* because of their emphasis on the need for a stable monetary policy) who contended that fiscal policy cannot possibly achieve the social benefits attributed to it by Keynes and his followers. However, most of the attention of professional economists during the 1960s was directed at finding effective means of expanding total demand in the economy. Little attention was given to the supply side of the macroeconomic equation and how taxes and government expenditures affected total supply and, therefore, employment and unemployment.

The 1970s were a period of "stagflation," a time during which the Nixon, Ford, and Carter administrations faced the twin problems of inflation and stagnation in national income and employment. It became apparent to a growing number of economists during the period that Keynesian economics did not provide readymade solutions for all of the problems associated with stagflation. Indeed, many wondered if there were not stringent tradeoffs to be made between solving the problems of inflation and unemployment. The search began for new ways of looking at the problems facing the macroeconomy of the 1970s. This reading deals with one of the new ways of thinking about policy. It deals with the development in the 1970s of what has come to be called the Laffer curve, named after its originator, economist Arthur Laffer at the University of Southern California. As we will see, this reading is also concerned with the influence government tax policy has on individual incentives to work, save, and invest and, therefore, on the national income and employment levels. Briefly, the chapter deals with the supply, rather than the demand, in the macroeconomy.

TAXES AND INCENTIVES ONCE AGAIN

Keynesian economic theory implicitly assumes a direct relationship between the rates at which incomes are taxed (i.e., tax rates) and total tax collections of the federal government. As we have seen, this view of the relationship between tax rates and tax collection leads to the conclusion that economic activity can be stimulated by a reduction in tax rates: lower tax rates mean more purchasing power for consumers, more purchases and greater consumption demand, more production and national income, and less unemployment. Further, the view leads to the conclusion that inflation can be suppressed by an appropriate increase in the tax rates: higher tax rates spell more taxes for the government and less purchasing for the consumer, fewer purchases by consumers, lower consumption demand, and the elimination of any excess demand in the economy that is putting upward pressure on prices. To repeat an important point, Keynesian economics is designed to deal with problems of unemployment and inflation through changes in demand.

In addition to their effects on aggregate demand in the economy, Arthur Laffer emphasizes that tax rates can have important effects on the supply of goods and services in the macroeconomy. This is because tax rates affect people's incentives to work and produce the goods and services that give rise to income. Up to a point, higher tax rates can lead to greater effort on the part of people as they attempt to offset, by way of more earnings, the effects of taxes on their purchasing power. However, Laffer reasons that there is some point beyond which higher tax rates can actually reduce the amount of time people spend at work and, thereby, reduce the national supply of goods and services.

Higher tax rates not only reduce people's purchasing power, but they also reduce the value of work and reduce the cost people have to incur when they forgo an hour of work and engage in leisure-time activities, like riding a bicycle, going fishing, or just talking with friends. Higher tax rates effectively reduce the price of leisure (since less is given up for an hour of leisure), inducing people to take more leisure—less work. (Remember the law of demand?)

These points are further developed in Figure 3–1. In that figure we have scaled income along the vertical axis and hours of leisure along the horizontal axis. The typical citizen-taxpayer has, let us suppose, some amount of time, like T_4 or 60 hours per week, that he or she can use for work or play. If he or she uses the time for work, a money income is earned and benefits are received indirectly through the goods that can be bought. How much money income is earned for the amount of leisure time forgone is dependent upon the individual's wage rate in the market. If a citizen-taxpayer uses the time for play, benefits are received directly from the activities. The individual can give up leisure for money income, giving up the direct benefits of leisure in the process for benefits received indirectly from the purchase of goods and services with money income. In other words, in terms of Figure 3–1, the individual has a transformation curve that extends from a point on the horizontal axis, like T_4, to a point on the vertical axis, like M_8 or $600 per week (assuming the wage rate is $10 per hour of work).

FIGURE 3–1

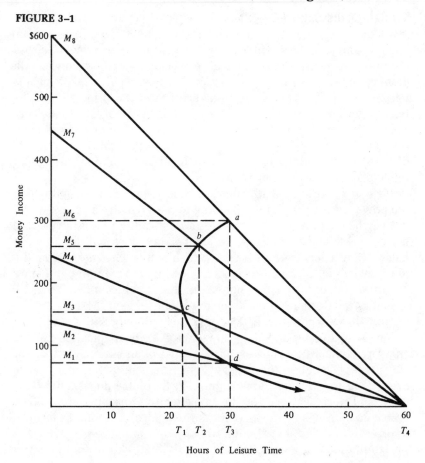

Hours of Leisure Time

Without any taxes being applied to money income, the individual can move from position T_4 to a position like a on the transformation curve. In moving to a, the individual gives up 30 hours of leisure for $300 per week in income. The individual could have more money but presumably the additional goods are not worth the additional hours of leisure that must be forgone.

Suppose the government imposes a 25 percent tax on money income. Such a tax means that the individual will take home $7.50 [$10 − .25 ($10)] for each hour worked. The tax also means that the price the individual pays for using an hour for some activity like talking with friends is reduced from $10 (which is the price without the tax) to $7.50 (which is the price after the tax is imposed). Embedded in the imposed tax are two effects: (1) an "income effect" revealed in the citizen's reduced purchasing power (or after-tax income) and (2) a "price effect" revealed in the lower price of leisure (and the higher price of goods and services than can be bought with money). With a tax rate of 25 percent, the income effect, which leads to greater work, may be more powerful than the price effect. The result: the taxpayer works longer and has fewer hours for leisure time activities. Graphically, the citizen-taxpayer moves from position a (which is on the transformation curve that reflects a tax rate of zero) to position b (which is on the transformation curve that reflects a tax rate of 25 percent).

If the tax rate is raised further, there is some point beyond which the power of the price effect (leading to more leisure and less work) outweighs the power of the income effect (leading to less leisure and more work). The consequence of higher tax rates will then be, on balance, more leisure and less work. The reduced hours spent on the job spell less output and less income in the macroeconomy. In Figure 3–1, more leisure is taken when the higher tax rates move the individual's transformation curve below M_4T_4 to, say, M_2T_4.

How do we know that higher tax rates will eventually lead to an increase in the amount of leisure, you ask. Your question can be answered by considering the consequences of an extreme tax rate of 100 percent. Under such a heavy tax rate, the government takes everything the worker earns in money; there are no benefits from work and no incentives for the taxpayer to work for money. The taxpayer then has every incentive to use all of his time in leisure-time activities. Graphically, the transformation curve lies along the horizontal axis in Figure 3–1. The individual chooses 60 hours of leisure and no hours of work, or combination e. To move from a point like c (when the tax rate is less than 100 percent) to point e (when the tax rate is 100 percent), the individual must move through combinations like d that represent fewer hours of work.

The same kind of analysis can be applied to the effects that higher and higher tax rates have on people's incentive to save and invest. Higher tax rates reduce the benefits received from not consuming (saving) and from taking the risks associated with investment. Up to a point, higher tax rates can spur saving and investment (since people can then try to offset the negative income effects of the higher tax rates by saving more and taking more risks). However, as in the case of taxes on income earned from work, higher tax rates can, beyond some point, reduce the benefits of saving and investing so severely that people save and invest less. The reduced investment means a lower capital stock for future generations and lower incomes than otherwise in the future (since less capital will mean lower productivity for workers).

The total tax collections (T) of the government are a function of two key variables: the tax rate (r) and income (Y). The mathematical relationship can be easily stated:

$$T = rY$$

For some increase in the tax rate (r), the income level (Y) can rise, giving rise to greater tax collections for the government. However, as we have pointed out, there is some increase in the tax rates that can have perverse effects on the income level: income can fall to such an extent that the product of r and Y, which is tax collections, actually falls.[1]

We noted in the preceding chapter that tax rates not only influence people's choices between work and leisure but also influence the form of income that is earned. Specifically, higher tax rates encourage people to take larger and larger shares of their incomes in nontaxable fringe benefits. High tax rates also induce people to move their work into the subterranean economy. In summary, tax collections of the government can, beyond some tax-rate level, be depressed due to (1) lower actual income and (2) lower reported taxable income.

With this knowledge of the incentive effects of tax rates, Laffer has devised a simple curve—the Laffer curve—that describes the relationship between tax rates and tax collections of the government. The general shape of the curve is illustrated in Figure 3–2. Initially, as tax rates in the figure rise from r_1 to r_2, tax collections of the government rise from T_1 to T_2. However, beyond r_2, taxable and reported incomes fall, resulting in an actual reduction in the tax collections of the government. At r_4 tax collections are zero.

THE LAFFER CURVE AND TAX POLICY

The Laffer curve has two important features. First, for every tax-collection level other than T_2 there are two tax rates—a high one and a low one—that yield the same revenue to the government. For instance, a tax rate of r_1 results in a tax collection of T_1, as indi-

---

[1] If the tax rate is raised from 30 to 40 percent and taxable income falls from $2.2 trillion to $1.6 trillion, tax collections fall from $660 billion to $640 billion.

FIGURE 3–2

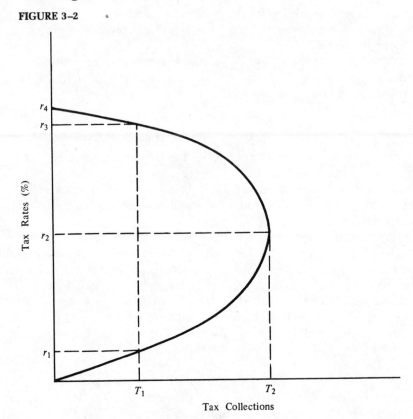

Tax Collections

cated above. However, a much higher tax rate, r_3, yields the exact same tax revenue. If given the choice between tax rates of r_1 and r_3, any government interested in maximizing its own welfare *and* the welfare of the public it is supposed to serve will choose r_1. The lower tax rate is certainly more desirable to taxpayers (aside from those with rather perverse preferences!), and it provides revenues for the same level of government programs as does the higher tax rate.

Second, as suggested in Figure 3–2, the impact of a tax rate increase depends critically upon the current *level* of taxation (as well as other factors). If tax rates are relatively low, then an increase in them will result in an expansion of tax revenues and of the ability of government to conduct its business. However, if the current level of tax rates is above r_2, an increase in rates can cause a reduction in government revenues and, accordingly, a contraction in government programs. Taxpayers are obviously hurt by such a rate increase, since they are then on lower utility levels. In addition, beneficiaries of government programs (like welfare recipients and military officers) are also harmed, since a cutback in programs can be a consequence of a reduction in tax revenues.

Observations regarding the effects of a tax-rate decrease are just as important. A tax-rate reduction can, at low levels of taxation, lead to lower tax collections and government expenditures. However, at very high levels of taxation, a tax-rate reduction can lead to an expansion of government. Under the latter condition, everyone presumably will benefit: lower tax rates will enhance taxpayer welfare. In addition, the lower tax rates will give the government the wherewithal to expand its programs and benefit people. The rate reduction will also give people greater incentive to work, save, and invest. The consequence is an expansion of national income and employment opportunities.

Professor Laffer and Congressman Jack Kemp and William Roth see in the Laffer curve a perspective for government fiscal policy that stands in sharp contrast with the Keynesian perspective. As we discussed, Keynesian economics leads to the conclusion that unemployment and sluggish national income growth can be alleviated by tax-rate cuts: tax-rate cuts lead to more consumer and business purchases—to greater aggregate demand. Laffer, Kemp, and Roth suggest that this Keynesian policy proposal not only has a questionable theoretical foundation but also is not very practical in times of high rates of inflation, such as the 1970s. Greater aggregate demand, without a change in the supplies of goods and services, can only contribute to inflationary pressures.

Laffer, Kemp, and Roth contend that tax rates should be reduced for the purposes of affecting the aggregate supply of goods. Tax-rate reductions will give people a greater incentive to work and produce, and the greater income earned from production will give people the means of buying the output. Further, they are convinced that, under the present tax system, tax rates in general are above r_2. Therefore, a tax-rate reduction will also have the effect of increasing tax collections of government. Therefore, a tax-rate reduction is good because it benefits both taxpayers and government.

The general shape of the Laffer curve is not a matter of dispute among policymakers and economists. On the other hand, there is considerable professional dispute over where we, as a nation, are on the Laffer curve. Stated differently, there is substantial disagreement over whether current tax rates in the United States are, on average, above or below r_2. The issue—which is really an empirical one—is important because of the consequences that a general tax-rate reduction will have on tax collections of government and on the ability of the government to develop its defense capability and to foster social-welfare programs. If we are above r_2, a tax-rate reduction will lead to higher tax collections. But if we are below r_2, a tax rate reduction will have the opposite effect.

Unfortunately, only a few, limited studies have been done on the supply-side effects of tax-rate reductions. The estimates that have been made are contradictory. In short, we just do not know whether tax collections will rise or fall with rate reductions. We suspect that the directional movement of tax collections will, in the final analysis, depend critically upon the type of taxes that are reduced (business and corporate income taxes and/or personal income taxes), the size of the general tax reduction, and the change in the structure of the tax-rate system.

SUPPLY-SIDE ECONOMICS AND INFLATION

Under Keynesian economics, inflation is viewed as a product of too much aggregate demand in the economy, or more goods being demanded than there are goods being produced. The difference between aggregate demand and aggregate supply places upward pressures on prices in general. Hence, Keynesians believe that inflation in the economy can be reduced by a decrease in aggregate demand. And the federal government can reduce the total demand of consumers, businesses, and governments in three principal ways: (1) a reduction in government expenditures, keeping taxes constant (and, when appropriate, running a budgetary surplus); (2) an increase in taxes by way of an increase in tax rates, holding government expenditures constant; and (3) a decrease in government expenditures along with an increase in taxes.

Supply-side economists tend to be monetarists; that is, they believe that the overwhelmingly important determinant of short-run demand in the economy is the money stock. They do not believe that government fiscal policy can do very much to affect short-run aggregate demand (at least in the way and to the extent Keynesians believe). If government reduces its expenditures and/or increases its tax collections, then monetarists argue the government will simply be less active in borrowing funds in the bond market. The lower demand for funds will lead to lower interests and greater investments and greater demand by businesses. The reduced demand brought about by government fiscal actions will be largely offset by greater demand in other sectors of the economy.

Supply-side economists, on the other hand, argue (as we have stressed above) that inflation can be fought by a reduction in tax rates—a policy recommendation that is diametrically opposite the Keynesian policy conclusion. The lower tax rates will lead to more production. And so long as the money stock is held constant, greater production will mean that the same number of dollars are chasing a larger quantity of goods and the overall price level should fall. If the money stock is growing at a constant rate that exceeds the rate of growth in output (at given tax rates), the economy will, of course, be experiencing inflation (since more dollars will then be chasing after relatively fewer goods). Under these circumstances, however, the greater production brought about by the lower tax rates should temper inflationary pressures—that is, should lower the inflation rate. In short, tax rate reductions "kill two birds with one stone," the production and unemployment problem and the inflation problem.

The reader should understand that the Keynesians have not yet, and for good reason, conceded the last word in the debate over appropriate anti-inflation tax policy to the supply-side economists. Keynesians may agree that lower tax rates will spur production, but they still point to the possibility that tax-rate cuts affect aggregate demand through increases in people's after-tax incomes. Whether or not inflation is quelled by a tax-rate cut depends upon the timing and relative magnitudes of the aggregate demand and aggregate supply effects. Given the tax-rate reduction, the demand effect may be larger than the supply effect, leading to greater inflationary pressures in the short and, possibly, long run. Further, Keynesians may point to the very real possibility that the supply effects of rate cuts may not occur until sometime in the future (when people are finally able to respond to the greater incentive of tax-rate cuts); but the demand effect may be almost immediate, meaning that rate cuts lead to greater inflationary pressures in the short run.

Supply-side economists are left unperturbed by the foregoing arguments. They might argue that even if the demand arguments of Keynesians turn out to be correct, the appropriate fiscal policy of the government may still be to lower (not raise) tax rates. Keynesians want to reduce aggregate demand by increasing government tax collections. If the average tax rate of people and businesses is above r_2 in Figure 3–2 and if tax rates are raised, then government will collect fewer, not more, taxes. Fewer goods will be produced (because of the negative incentive effects of the rate hike), and more income will go unreported to the IRS. The consequence: greater inflationary pressures, even following the Keynesian model of the macroeconomy. The Keynesians might retort by stressing that tax rates are, on average, below r_2 in Figure 3–2.

Where or when will the argument be settled? We wish we could answer that question. Much conceptual and empirical work remains to be done, as we have said. Our only advice is to stay tuned to subsequent editions of this book; perhaps we will be able to give you the answer if the issue is, in fact, ever settled.

SUPPLY-SIDE ECONOMICS: THE RICH VERSUS THE POOR

The discussion above has been developed in terms of an average tax rate for the entire population. We know, however, that tax rates vary across income groups. What constitutes appropriate tax policy for government (to accomplish whatever objective is set for government) depends critically upon the *structure* of taxes and the reaction of various groups to changes in their particular taxes. Again, consider the Laffer curve depicted this time in Figure 3–3. The United States operates under a progressive tax-rate system. This means that the higher the income, generally speaking, the higher the tax rate. Just for purposes of illustration, suppose the United States tax code is so constructed that the tax rates of high-income groups (the rich) are quite high and at position R on the Laffer curve. Suppose further that the tax rates of low income groups (the poor) are rather low and at position P on the Laffer curve.

Several points are apparent from the situation developed. An across-the-board, uniform cut in tax rates may indeed have all the incentive effects that supply-side economists contend will occur. However, it does not follow necessarily that the tax collections of the federal government will rise. The tax collections from the rich may rise, but the tax collections of the poor may fall and fall by more or less than the rise in the tax collections from the rich. However, this does not mean that the poor should necessarily be against tax-rate reductions for the rich. Such tax-rate reductions can conceivably lead to higher tax revenues that will enable the government to lower the tax rates of the poor. The government may or may not be able to lower the tax rates of the poor by as much as the rich, but both groups can still be better off. The economy can operate more efficiently and the government can maintain its current level of services.

Finally, we might note that analysis of government tax policy by way of the Laffer curve may suggest some rather odd and interest-

FIGURE 3-3

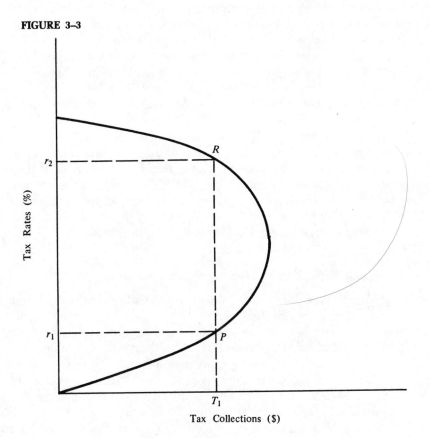

Tax Collections ($)

ing political proposals for Keynesian economists. Let us suppose that Keynesians believe the Laffer curve looks the way it does in Figure 3–3 (as we mentioned, no economist really questions the general shape of the curve), that inflation is prevalent in the economy, and that we want to formulate appropriate Keynesian policy recommendations to combat inflation. How do we do that? As we said before, we want to raise tax collections. However, a uniform increase in everyone's tax rates may not lead to higher tax collections. In terms of Figure 3–3, the tax collections of the poor will rise when their rates are raised above r_1. However, tax collections of the rich will fall if their tax rates are raised above r_2. The result of a uniform, across-the-board tax-rate increase may indeed be an increase in tax collections: the increase in the tax collections from the poor is greater than the decrease in tax collections from the rich.

The main problem with the uniform rate increase is that in order to increase government revenue by a given amount, the tax rates on the poor will have to be greater than they need to be.

Indeed, if the government wants to increase tax collections from all groups (or if the government wants to minimize the increase in the tax collections from the poor) then it should *raise* the tax rates of the *poor* and *lower* the tax rates of the *rich*. Of course, the conditions that underlie the analysis and lead to this conclusion may never really hold in the economy. Our point is that they *could* exist for some times and for some economies and that these are the types of policy conclusions that may be drawn from future research. If they are, we can only wonder how the electorate will receive the tax proposals and how well (or not so well) politicians who advocate such proposals will fair in elections. Supply-side economics may make for some very interesting political campaigns in the future.

CONCLUDING COMMENTS

Economics is fraught with controversy. Nowhere in the discipline is that truism more readily apparent than in macroeconomics and the growing debate between demand-side and supply-side economists. Both groups of economists have similar, if not identical, objectives —the reduction of unemployment and inflation. However as we have seen in this chapter, the two groups have distinctly different perspectives on how policy affects the economy. Hence, the two groups often make policy recommendations that are at odds with one another. For instance, to cure inflation demand-side Keynesian economists recommend tax-rate increases. Supply-side economists recommend just the opposite, tax-rate decreases. The debate on the issue vividly illustrates how important empirical studies are to the development of public policy. Because of the limitations of empirical studies, on the other hand, the debate may never be satisfactorily resolved.

READING 4

Who's in Charge Here?

Monetary policy is the responsibility of the Federal Reserve, but to whom is the Federal Reserve responsible?

The answer to that question is so complex that if we unravel it successfully (which is not too likely a prospect), we will either have unveiled one of the great socioeconomic creations in the annals of civilization, comparable to the invention of inside plumbing, or unmasked one of the most devious schemes ever contrived by the mind of man to camouflage the true locus of clandestine power.

According to some, the Federal Reserve is responsible to the Congress. But it is the President, not Congress, who appoints the seven members of the Board of Governors of the Federal Reserve System who occupy the stately building at 20th Street and Constitution Avenue, Washington, D.C. The President also selects from among those seven the Chairman of the Board of Governors, the principal spokesman for the central bank.

On that basis, one might surmise that the Federal Reserve is responsible to the executive branch of government, in the person of the President and his (or her) administration. However, since each member serves a fourteen-year term, the current President can appoint only two of the seven-member Board of Governors, unless there are deaths or resignations. Even the Chairman may be the appointee of the previous administration. Furthermore, it is Congress that created the

Federal Reserve (not in its own image) in 1913, and it is Congress, not the President, that has the authority to alter its working mandate at any time. In 1935, for example, Congress chose to throw two administration representatives off the Board of Governors—namely, the Secretary of the Treasury and the Comptroller of the Currency, both of whom had been ex officio members—simply because they were representatives of the executive branch.

Others, more cynical, have suggested that the Federal Reserve is mostly responsible to the private banking community, primarily the 5,600 commercial banks that are member banks of the Federal Reserve System. The member banks do in fact choose the presidents of each of the twelve regional Federal Reserve banks, including the president of the most aristocratic of all, the Federal Reserve Bank of New York. It may or may not be significant that the annual salary of the President of the Federal Reserve Bank of New York is $110,-000, while that of the Chairman of the Board of Governors in Washington is $57,500.

Who's in charge here? Who, indeed?

Formal Structure

The statutory organization of the Federal Reserve System is a case study in those currently popular concepts, decentralization and the blending of public and private authority. A deliberate attempt was made in the enabling congressional legislation (the 1913 Federal Reserve Act) to diffuse power over a broad base—geographically; between the private and public sectors; and even within the government—so that no one person, group, or sector, either inside or outside the government, could exert enough leverage to dominate the thrust of monetary policy.

As noted in the organizational diagram on the next page, the Board of Governors of the Federal Reserve System consists of seven members, appointed by the President with the advice and consent of the Senate. To prevent presidential board-packing, each member is appointed for a term of fourteen years, with one term expiring at the end of January in each even-numbered year. Furthermore, no two board members may come from the same Federal Reserve District. The Chairman of the Board of Governors, chosen from among the seven by the President, serves a four-year term. However, his term is not concurrent with the presidential term, so an incoming President could find himself saddled with an already appointed Chairman for part of his first term in office. The Board is independent of the congressional appropriations process and partially exempt from audit by the government's watchdog, the General Accounting Office, since its operating funds come from the earnings of the twelve regional Federal Reserve Banks.

The regional Federal Reserve Banks, one in each Federal Reserve District, are geographically dispersed throughout the nation—the Federal Reserve Bank of New York, the Federal Reserve Bank of Kansas City, the Federal Reserve Bank of San Francisco, and so on. Each Federal Reserve Bank is privately owned by the member banks in its district, the very commercial banks it is charged with supervising and regulating. Each member commercial bank is required to buy stock in its district Federal Reserve Bank equal to 6 percent of its own capital and surplus. Of this 6 percent, 3 percent must be paid in and 3 percent is subject to call by the Board of Governors. However, the profits accruing to ownership are limited by law to a 6 percent annual dividend on paid-in capital stock. The member bank stockholders elect six of the nine directors of their district Federal Reserve Bank, and the remaining three are appointed from Washington by the Board of Governors. These nine directors, in turn, choose the president of their Federal Reserve Bank, subject to the approval of the Board of Governors.

The directors of each Federal Reserve Bank also select a person, always a commercial banker, to serve on the Federal Advisory Council, a statutory body consisting of a member

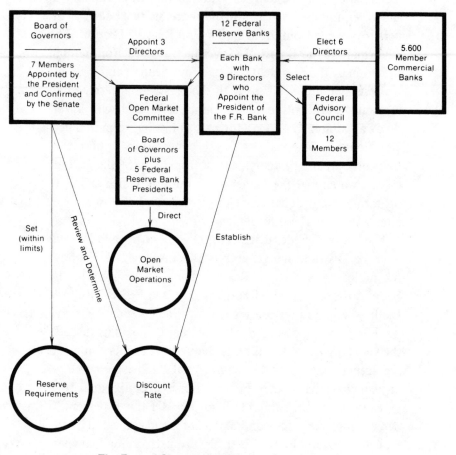

**The Formal Structure and Policy Organization of
the Federal Reserve System**

from each of the twelve Federal Reserve districts. The Federal Advisory Council consults quarterly with the Board of Governors in Washington and makes recommendations regarding the conduct of monetary policy.

Legal authority is similarly diffused with respect to the *execution* of monetary policy, as the diagram indicates. The Board of Governors has the power to set reserve requirements on commercial bank time and demand deposits, for example, but it cannot set them outside the bounds of the specific limits imposed by Congress (between 3 and 10 percent for time deposits, between 7 and 22 percent for demand deposits).

Open market operations are directed by a body known as the Federal Open Market Committee (FOMC), composed of the seven-member Board of Governors plus five of the Reserve Bank presidents. Since the members of the Board of Governors are appointed by the White House, and the Reserve Bank presidents are appointed by the directors of each Federal Reserve Bank, who are (six of nine) elected by the member commercial banks, the diffusion of authority over open market operations spans the distance from the White House to the member bank on Main Street. In addition, although the FOMC directs open market operations, they are executed at the trading desk of the Federal Reserve Bank of New York by a person who appears to be simultaneously an employee of the FOMC and the Federal Reserve Bank of New York.

Legal authority over discount rates is even more confusing. Discount rates are "established" every two weeks by the directors of each regional Federal Reserve Bank, but they are subject to "review and determination" by the Board of Governors. The distinction between "establishing" discount rates and "determining" them is a fine line indeed, and it would not be surprising if confusion occasionally arose as to precisely where the final authority and responsibility lie.

The Realities of Power

So much for the Land of Oz. Actually, the facts of life are rather different, as the more realistic diagram, which appears below, illustrates.

By all odds, the dominant figure in the formation and execution of monetary policy is the Chairman of the Board of Governors of the Federal Reserve System, currently Paul A. Volcker. He is the most prominent member of the board itself, the most influential member of the FOMC, and generally recognized by both Congress and the public at large as *the* spokesman for the Federal Reserve System. Although the Federal Reserve Act appears to put all seven members of the Board of Governors on a more or less equal footing, over the past fifty years the strong personalities, outstanding abilities, and determined devotion to purpose of the Chairmen—first Marriner S. Eccles, then William McChesney Martin, later Arthur F. Burns, and now Paul Volcker—have made them rather more equal than the others. As adviser to the President, negotiator with Congress, and final authority on appointments throughout the system, with influence over all aspects of monetary policy in his capacity as Chairman of both the Board of Governors and the FOMC, the Chairman for all practical purposes is the embodiment of the central bank in this country.

The other six members of the Board of Governors also exercise a substantial amount of authority, more so than is indicated in the formal paper structure of the system, because with the passage of time primary responsibility for monetary policy has become more centralized and concentrated in Washington. When the Federal Reserve Act was passed in 1913, it was thought that the Federal Reserve System would be mainly a passive service agency, supplying currency when needed, clearing checks, and providing a discount facility for the convenience of the private commercial member banks. At that time there was no conception of monetary policy as an active countercyclical force. Open

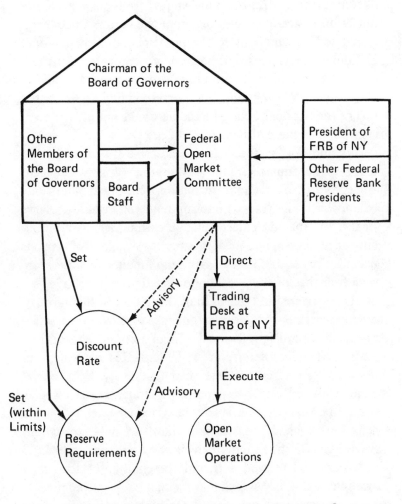

The Realities of Power within the Federal Reserve System

market operations were unknown and reserve requirements were fixed by law, with no flexibility permitted. Since then, of course, the central bank has shifted from passive accommodation to active regulation, from the performance of regional service functions to the implementation of national economic policy. This shift has been accompanied, naturally enough, by a rise in the power of the centralized Board of Governors in Washington and a corresponding decline in the role of the regional Federal Reserve Banks and their "owners," the commercial banks.

It would not be unrealistic to describe the central bank today as headquartered in Washington, with twelve field offices located throughout the nation. These field offices may be known by the rather imposing name of Federal Reserve Banks, and they do indeed retain a certain degree of autonomy in expressing their views on the wisdom of various policies. But even so they essentially amount to little more than branches of the Washington headquarters.

Closely related to the Board of Governors in the informal power structure, and deriving influence through that association, is the Board's professional staff of economic experts and advisers. The long tenure in the Federal Reserve System of many senior staff economists, their familiarity with Federal Reserve history, and their expertise in monetary analysis give them a power base that is to a large extent founded on the respect with which they, as individuals, are held throughout the system. Through daily consultation with the individual governors and written and oral presentations before each meeting of the FOMC, staff personnel exert an indefinable but significant influence on the ultimate decision-making process. In fact, in recent years three members of the Board's staff (Robert Holland, Charles Partee, and Lyle Gramley) have been elevated to the Board itself, via presidential nomination. It is also worth noting, by the way, that in 1978 Nancy Teeters became the first woman member of the Board of Governors. The first black member of the Board was Andrew Brimmer, who was appointed in 1966.

Aside from the Board of Governors, its Chairman and its

staff, the only other body playing a major role in Federal Reserve policy making is the Federal Open Market Committee, which meets every four weeks in Washington. Of the twelve members on the FOMC, a majority of seven are the Board of Governors themselves. The other five are Reserve Bank presidents. The President of the Federal Reserve Bank of New York is a permanent member of the FOMC, and the other eleven Federal Reserve Bank presidents alternate the remaining four seats among themselves.

The statutory authority of the FOMC is confined to the direction of open market operations, but in recent years it has become the practice to bring all policy matters under review at FOMC meetings. Although only five of the Reserve Bank presidents are entitled to vote at any one time, typically all twelve attend every meeting and participate in the discussion. Thus, potential reserve-requirement and discount-rate changes are, in effect, decided upon within the FOMC, with the twelve Reserve Bank presidents participating in an advisory capacity. The Board of Governors, however, always has the final say on reserve requirements and discount rates if matters should come to a showdown, particularly since legal opinion appears to be that in case of disagreement the Board's power to "review and determine" discount rates overrides the authority of the individual Reserve Banks to "establish" them.

Once the Federal Open Market Committee decides on the appropriate open market policy, actual execution of the policy directive until the next meeting is the responsibility of the account manager at the Federal Reserve Bank of New York's trading desk. He is called the account manager because he manages the System Open Market Account, which includes all of the securities holdings of the Federal Reserve System. Since the FOMC's instructions are often couched in rather broad language, the account manager has to translate these instructions into actual daily purchases and sales of Treasury securities. In the process, at least a modest amount of leeway and personal interpretation is inevitable, as we discuss further in Reading 6.

Like the account manager, the unique position of the President of the Federal Reserve Bank of New York in the hierarchy also stems from his role and status in the nation's financial center. If he is inclined to use this leverage, as Allan Sproul did a quarter century ago and Benjamin Strong before him, the President of the New York Reserve Bank can mount a substantial challenge even to the Chairman of the Board of Governors. Since such a challenge would have little legal foundation, it would have to be based on the prestige of the presidency of the Federal Reserve Bank of New York and the forcefulness of the man who holds the position. Both Allan Sproul and Benjamin Strong were men of exceptional ability and personality.

But where, in the corridors of power, does this leave the member banks, the directors of each Federal Reserve Bank, and the Federal Advisory Council? Pretty much shut out, if the truth be known.

The member banks do indeed "own" their district Federal Reserve Bank, but such stockholding is mostly symbolic and carries with it none of the usual attributes of ownership. The member banks also have a major voice in electing the directors of their Reserve Bank, but the directors in turn have responsibilities that are largely ceremonial. True, they appoint the members of the Federal Advisory Council, but the Federal Advisory Council serves mostly a public relations purpose and has little to do with actual policy making. The directors of each Federal Reserve Bank also choose the president of their Reserve Bank, subject to the approval of the Board of Governors. But the "subject to approval" clause has meant, in practice, that the most the directors can really do is submit a list of nominees for the position of president. On several occasions, the choice of the directors of a Federal Reserve Bank has not met with approval from Washington; such cases have made very clear exactly where ultimate authority is lodged.

How Independent the Central Bank?

The fact that ultimate authority over monetary policy resides in Washington brings to the fore the relationship between the central bank and the other branches of government also responsible for overall national economic policy—the Congress and the administration, the latter personified by the President.

The Federal Reserve is a creature of the Congress. The Constitution gives Congress the power "to coin money and regulate the value thereof." On this basis, in 1913 Congress created the Federal Reserve as the institution delegated to administer that responsibility on its behalf. Congress requires periodic accountability by the Federal Reserve and has the authority to amend the enabling legislation, the Federal Reserve Act, any time it sees fit.

Essentially, Congress has given the Federal Reserve a broad mandate to regulate the monetary system in the public interest and then has more or less stood aside and let the monetary authorities pursue this objective on their own and to the best of their abilities. Congress has also attempted to minimize interference on the part of the administration by giving each member of the Board of Governors a fourteen-year term, thereby sharply limiting any single President's influence over the board.

This semi-independent status of the central bank is a source of continuous friction. Some members of Congress believe that the Federal Reserve has carried its "independence" much too far. There has been some concern over its freedom from congressional appropriations and its partial exemption from standard government audit, as noted early in this chapter. Also, the Federal Reserve's responsibility on occasion for tight money and high interest rates has stimulated some intensive questioning at congressional hearings, including frequent scoldings of Federal Reserve officials by populist-minded congressmen who get uptight about tight money.

Others, in Congress and out, have complained that the Federal Reserve simply has not done a very good job, that we would all be better off if Congress laid down some guidelines or rules to limit the discretion available to the monetary authorities in conducting their business. We will discuss such proposals in Reading 7.

The relationship between the central bank and the President has also aroused considerable controversy. Many feel that the Federal Reserve should be a part of the executive branch of government, responsible to the President, on the grounds that monetary policy is an integral part of national economic policy. Monetary policy should therefore be coordinated at the highest level (that is, by the President), along with fiscal policy, as a component part of the administration's total program for economic growth and stability.

To do otherwise, it is charged, is both undemocratic and divisive. Undemocratic, because monetary policy is too important to be run by an elite group of experts insulated from the political process. Divisive, because monetary and fiscal policy should not work at cross-purposes. Since fiscal policy proposals are clearly within the President's domain, monetary policy should be as well. A Federal Reserve independent of presidential authority conflicts with the administration's responsibility to promulgate and coordinate an overall economic program.

On the other hand, the case for central bank independence from the President rests on the pragmatic grounds that subordination of the central bank to the executive branch of government invites excessive money creation and consequent inflation. The charge that an independent Federal Reserve is undemocratic is countered by the reminder that the central bank is still very much responsible to Congress, which can amend the Federal Reserve Act anytime it wishes. In addition, the President holds regular meetings with the Chairman of the Board of Governors, the Secretary of the Treasury, and the Chairman of the Council of Economic Advisers.

It is feared by many, and not without historical justification, that if the monetary authority is made the junior partner to the President or the Treasury (the fiscal authority), monetary stability will be sacrificed to the government's revenue needs—the government will be tempted to seek the easy way out in raising funds, by printing money or borrowing excessively at artificially low interest rates, in preference to the politically more difficult route of raising taxes or cutting back on government spending. The sole purpose of an independent monetary authority, in brief, is to forestall the natural propensity of governments to resort to inflation.

READING 5

Indicators and Instruments

In the good old days, when government agencies told us only what was good for us, the Federal Reserve told us nothing. Does that mean the Fed was engaged in undercover activities —like bugging bank tellers? Quite the contrary, says the Fed. Always reluctant to antagonize the Wizards of Wall Street, the Fed simply wanted to make sure that the financial experts had something to keep themselves busy. And what could serve better than trying to figure out what the Fed was up to? If the Fed told everyone in plain English what kind of monetary policy was on stage and in the wings, what would the multitude of Fed watchers in the financial community do to occupy their time?

Actually, there never was anything cloak-and-dagger about the Federal Reserve. It has always poured forth an alarming volume of reports, pamphlets, magazines, mono-graphs, and books that explained what central banking was all about. Guided tours and speakers were provided free of charge. Fed personnel were always delighted to discuss in detail why and how they did what they did—one, two, or ten years ago. But the *one* thing they were always reluctant to talk about—like central bankers throughout the world—was what they were doing at the moment and what they were planning to do next.

The Fed continues to behave as it always has so far as pamphlets, magazines, and monographs are concerned. But now, under congressional pressure, it must announce its intentions with respect to monetary policy: to be specific, periodically the Fed now announces its money supply targets for the coming year. Nevertheless, Fed watchers in banks and on Wall Street are busier than ever. Evidently what the Fed says and what it does are not necessarily the same thing! So join with us now in a thrilling adventure through the Federal Reserve Forest, as we search for that most elusive of animals: a reliable guide that will tell us what the Fed is really up to. Keep your eyes and ears open and be ever-alert for bear traps, false bottoms, and other unexpected tricks of the trade.

How Important Is the Discount Rate?

To judge by the press, many financial observers rely on movements in the discount rate to indicate the current stance and future course of monetary policy. A change in the discount rate is heralded on the front page of the *New York Times* and solemnly announced in respectful tones on the evening news. It is implied that when the Federal Reserve raises the discount rate, tight money is being ushered in, and when the discount rate is lowered, easy money is entering from the wings.

On the other hand, most Federal Reserve officials and academic economists agree that the discount rate is the *least* powerful of all the monetary instruments, a follower rather than a leader of monetary policy. So what indicators should we study? In order to assess the importance or unimportance of the discount rate and other indicators of central bank actions and intentions, let us first examine discount policy in some detail and then compare it with the other major tools of monetary policy—open market operations and reserve requirements.

One of the primary functions of a central bank, perhaps *the* primary function, has always been to stand ready at all times to provide liquidity to the economy in case of financial stress or crisis. As the ultimate source of liquidity, the central bank is responsible for promptly supplying money on those rare but crucial occasions when the economy threatens to break down for lack of funds. For this reason, the central bank has traditionally been called the "lender of last resort" in emergency situations. In more ordinary circumstances, it also lends funds to banks that are temporarily short of reserves. When the central bank lends, for whatever purpose, the rate of interest it charges is called the discount rate.

The discount rate was considered the main instrument of central banking throughout the nineteenth century and for the first three decades of the twentieth. It reached its apogee in prestige in 1931, when England's Macmillan Committee, somewhat carried away by the splendor of it all, reported that the discount rate "is an absolute necessity for the sound management of a monetary system, and is a most delicate and beautiful instrument for the purpose."

The long tradition behind discounting and the corollary importance of the discount rate stem from the fact that until the mid–1920s it was virtually the only means available to the central bank to accomplish its purposes. Now, of course, with other instruments also at the Federal Reserve's disposal, the relative role of discounting has declined noticeably.

It should be mentioned at the outset that discount policy has two dimensions: one is *price,* the discount rate, the rate of interest the Federal Reserve charges commercial banks when they borrow from the Fed; the other is Federal Reserve surveillance over the *amount* that each bank is borrowing. Thus, one obvious flaw in using the discount rate alone as an indicator of monetary policy is that the rate might remain unchanged while the Federal Reserve employs more stringent (or more lenient) surveillance procedures. Monetary policy could thereby become tighter or easier, even through discount policy, but without any change in the discount rate.

The objective of raising the discount rate is just what the Federal Reserve says it is: to discourage commercial banks from borrowing at the Federal Reserve. When banks borrow from the Federal Reserve, their reserves increase and on that foundation they can expand their loans and investments and thereby the money supply. Less borrowing at the Federal Reserve because of a higher discount rate thus means less bank lending to business, smaller growth in the money supply, and higher interest rates generally.

This process, it should be noted, provides no *direct* connection between changes in the discount rate and changes in market interest rates. The effects of a change in the discount rate are seen as operating through the mechanism of changes in bank reserves and the money supply, just as is the case with open market operations and changes in reserve requirements. (However, as we point out in the next section, the magnitude of the effect on reserves of a change in the discount rate has been minute, compared with the reserve effects of the two other tools available to the Federal Reserve.)

And yet, there does appear to be a connection between the discount rate and market interest rates. As can be seen in the

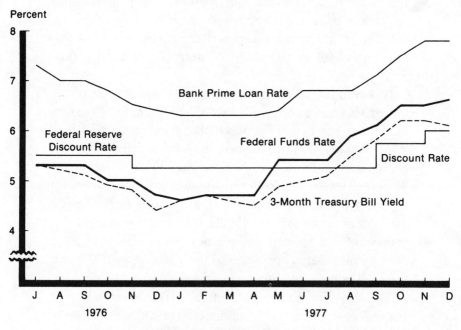

Togetherness 1976–1977

following diagram, a close relationship exists between the discount rate and interest rates on short-term money-market instruments, such as Treasury bills and Federal funds (the rate on overnight loans of reserves between banks), and also between the discount rate and the prime bank lending rate (the interest rate that banks charge their best business customers).

Note that the diagram shows that there is no fixed relationship between the discount rate and other money market yields. Sometimes the discount rate is above the Treasury-bill yield and the Federal funds rate and sometimes it is below them. Moreover, careful examination reveals that changes in Treasury-bill yields typically *precede* changes in the discount rate. Treasury-bill yields rise, probably because of Federal Reserve open market operations, and then—after they have risen quite a while and often quite a bit—the discount rate moves up. Or bill rates fall and then the discount rate is lowered. In other words, a change in the discount rate is likely to come *after* a basic switch in monetary policy has already occurred; it verifies the switch and reinforces it, but does not signal it.

Discount rate as a lagging indicator.

One possible way that changes in the discount rate might directly affect market interest rates is through the "announcement effect" produced when a discount-rate change comes unexpectedly. An unanticipated rise in the discount rate is likely to lead bondholders to expect tight money and higher interest rates (lower bond prices). They sell bonds to avoid capital losses, thus hastening the drop in bond prices and the rise in interest rates.

The key, of course, is that the rise in the discount rate under such circumstances generates expectations regarding future interest rates. But if the public had already observed tightening in the credit markets prior to the change in the discount rate, the actual announcement itself would produce very little reaction. In fact, the bond markets might be relieved of uncertainty, and interest rates might fall.

In any event, the bulk of the evidence suggests that while there may be some cause-and-effect connection between changes in the discount rate and changes in market interest rates, through expectations, for the most part the relationship is indirect—through changes in bank reserves and the money supply. It also bears repeating that typically a change in the discount rate comes after, not before, a basic shift in monetary policy. It confirms what is going on but does not anticipate it. As an indicator, therefore, it is comparable to a fighter who learns his opponent's right cross is on the way when it crashes into his nose.

In an effort to keep the discount rate in closer touch with other short-term rates, there was a change in the administration of the discount rate late in 1970. During the 1960s, changes in the discount rate were made rather infrequently, a pattern that was mirrored by the prime rate charged by commercial banks to their best customers. During the ten years from 1960 until 1970 the discount rate was changed a total of twelve times and the prime rate was changed a total of sixteen times. (In fact, much of the impact of tight money during that period was transmitted to the prime customers of banks by changes in compensating balances—the portion of a loan that must be held on deposit at the bank—that were required of business firms, and by changes in the standards as to who qualified for the prime rate. Thus, even the comovement in the discount rate and the prime rate was somewhat illusory, since the effective prime rate changed even though the posted rate remained fixed.)

To avoid the uncertain announcement effects associated with large and infrequent changes, late in 1970 the Federal Reserve embarked on a course of altering the discount rate more frequently and in smaller steps. During the fourteen months from November 1970 through December 1971, for example, the discount rate was changed eight times, only four less than during the entire 1960–70 period. Similarly, the prime rate was changed a total of twenty-three times during that period, seven more times than during the entire decade of the 1960s.

The discount rate now follows the movements in short-term rates, especially the Treasury bill rate and the Federal funds rate, even more closely than before. It is clear that the Federal Reserve prefers to get changes in the discount rate off the front pages of the *New York Times* and into the anonymity of the interest rate quotations in the financial section (which happens to be close to the sports pages, allowing you to throw away the first section of the paper). Some commercial banks have tied the prime rate to other short-term rates for similar reasons—so that the prime rate no longer has the appearance of an administered rate but rather moves up and down with impersonal market forces.

Discount Rate versus Reserve Requirements versus Open Market Operations

If changes in the discount rate exert their main effects via bank reserves and the money supply, it is relevant to compare them in this respect with the other tools of monetary policy—changes in reserve requirements and open market operations.

What proportion of member-bank reserves is attributable to the discounting process, to member banks' borrowing the reserves from the Federal Reserve? In 1950, total member-bank reserves were about $17 billion; less than half a billion of these reserves were acquired through the discount process. In 1979, member-bank reserves totaled about $40 billion; about $1.3 billion were due to borrowing from the Federal Reserve.

During the 1950s, 1960s and 1970s, borrowings from the Federal Reserve averaged about half a billion dollars annually. Even at its occasional peak levels, discounting never provided more than 10 percent of total bank reserves and usually the percentage was much less—on average about 2 or 3 percent.

The Federal Reserve does *not* use discount policy as a primary tool for changing bank reserves. For one thing, the initiative for discounting lies with the banks, not with the Federal Reserve. The Federal Reserve can lower the discount rate, but this does not force the banks to increase their borrowings. A change in the discount rate affects only those banks that are in debt to the Federal Reserve, or that consider such borrowing to be a likely source of funds. Many banks never borrow from the Federal Reserve except in dire emergency.

Reserve-requirement changes, on the other hand, have an extremely powerful impact on bank-reserve positions and the money supply. A small change in the required reserve ratio instantly produces a rather large change in bank excess reserves. Because the impact is so powerful, so blunt, so immediate, and so widespread, the Federal Reserve uses its authority to change reserve requirements only sparingly, particularly during tight money periods when increases in reserve requirements would be appropriate.

After all is said and done, the day-by-day standby of monetary policy, in good times and bad, is open market operations. The purchase or sale of government securities can be undertaken in large or small amounts, as the Federal Reserve chooses. The impact is fairly prompt; it is possible to proceed gradually and to reverse field rapidly.

One reason market interest rates change before the discount rate changes is precisely because the Federal Reserve has already been active with open market operations. When the Federal Reserve alters the direction of monetary policy, it is open market operations that typically lead the way. It is also open market operations that do the brunt of the work as the new policy gathers momentum, with back-up support where necessary and appropriate from the discount rate and reserve requirements.

A Pride of Lions, a Gaggle of Geese, and a Plethora of Indicators

Unfortunately, since open market operations are so unobtrusive, the search for reliable indicators of what the central bank is up to becomes more difficult than ever. The discount rate is generally not too helpful a guide to what the Federal Reserve is doing, except as confirmation of a change in monetary policy that has already occurred. A change in the direction of monetary policy can occur without any change in the discount rate, and conversely a change in the discount rate does not normally initiate a change in Federal Reserve policy.

Reserve requirement changes are not of much assistance because they are used so seldom. Paradoxically, open market operations are not very helpful for the opposite reason—they are used too frequently.

Weekly data on Federal Reserve open market operations are released every Friday afternoon and published in Saturday's papers. But the knowledge that the Federal Reserve bought or sold so many government securities during any one week, or even over a succession of weeks, is in itself of limited value; the transactions may have been made simply to offset some "outside" factors that were affecting bank reserves, such as a seasonal inflow of currency, changes in the Treasury's cash balances, or any of a multitude of other possibilities. (You can get more details on some of the mechanics of open market operations—if such things turn you on—in the next chapter.)

Since it is widely understood that weekly data on open market operations alone give an inadequate picture of what is going on, many financial observers rely more on movements in interest rates for clues to the current stance of monetary policy. Of all yields, the ones most quickly responsive to monetary policy are probably the rate on short-term Treasury bills and the Federal funds rate. The Federal funds rate is the rate charged on reserves lent from one bank to another. On any given day, some banks have excess reserves and other banks have reserve deficiencies. There are brokers who bring such banks together to arrange for a loan (called a purchase and sale) from banks with surplus reserves to banks with deficient reserves. The agreed upon interest rate is called the Federal funds rate. It can rise significantly when there are few banks with excess reserves and lots with reserve deficiencies, and it can drop just as precipitously when the reserve rich banks outnumber the poor. Thus it acts as a sensitive barometer of conditions in the reserves market.

However, as reliable indicators of what the central bank is doing, all interest rates have serious limitations. To Monetarists, who emphasize the money supply, they are irrelevant. Aside from that, it should be obvious that they are susceptible to change for reasons other than Federal Reserve policy; this makes it dangerous to read them as though they were determined exclusively by the Federal Reserve. The central bank has a substantial influence over the supply of credit, but only limited influence over the demand for it, so that interest rates may fluctuate for reasons that have nothing to do with the Federal Reserve's actions. Tight money generally means a rise in interest rates, but a rise in interest rates does not necessarily mean tight money. Indeed, because of inflation, excessively *easy* money might also produce a rise in interest rates.

Given the shortcomings of all the "orthodox" indicators —the discount rate, open market transactions, and the behavior of interest rates—the Federal Reserve, always helpful, releases a truckload of numbers each Friday afternoon along with the data on open market operations. It presents current statistics on a wide variety of alternative indicators. You can take your pick!

It lists weekly figures on all of the following: the monetary base, total member-bank reserves, the volume of member-bank discounting from the Federal Reserve, free reserves, various measures of the money supply, business loans at large commercial banks, and a few hundred other numbers just for good measure.

All these are self-explanatory except perhaps the monetary base and free reserves. The monetary base is defined as total member-bank reserves plus currency outstanding. Free reserves equals member-bank excess reserves less their borrowings from the Federal Reserve; when borrowings exceed excess reserves, it is usually called net borrowed reserves.

With this smorgasbord of indicators, plus the orthodox

ones that are on the back burner, you can select those that best suit your individual taste. As this discussion suggests, a Monetarist will lean toward the money supply in one form or another, a Keynesian toward interest rates and business loans. An eclectic will stuff himself on a little bit of everything, and if life becomes more complicated that way he has only himself to blame.

Free reserves attained some degree of popularity a few years ago but have fallen from favor. The main trouble is that a given level of free reserves is compatible with many different levels of the money supply and bank credit. The figure for free reserves has fluctuated within roughly the same limits for the past twenty years, while the money supply and bank credit have grown considerably during that interval.

At the same time as the Monetarists are downgrading interest rates as indicators of Federal Reserve policy, because they are not under the firm control of the central bank, Keynesians are saying the same thing about the money supply—that it is influenced by commercial bank behavior in conjunction with swings in economic activity, and that it can be controlled only imperfectly by the Federal Reserve. For example, as interest rates on bank loans and investments rise (relative to the discount rate) during a business upswing, banks borrow more from the discount window, expand their loans, and increase the money supply. Similarly, as interest rates fall, perhaps because of a slowdown in economic activity, banks repay their borrowings at the Federal Reserve, reduce their loans, and contract the money supply. If it is the central bank that is solely responsible for changes in the money supply, then it is a good indicator of Federal Reserve policy. But if the money supply can change regardless of Federal Reserve intentions, then using it as an indicator is likely to throw you off the track.

In order to save the money supply as an indicator of monetary policy, Monetarists Karl Brunner and Allan Meltzer have marshaled statistical evidence showing that it is Federal Reserve initiative—open market operations and reserve-requirement changes—that is the main cause of movements in the money supply. As a backup, however, they propose the monetary base as an alternative indicator, a first cousin to the money supply but somewhat more directly under the Federal Reserve's thumb.

Other Federal Reservologists prefer total reserves to the monetary base. For still others, including the architects of the Federal Reserve–MIT–Penn model, total reserves must be purged of reserves arising from member bank borrowing at the discount window—leaving us with nonborrowed reserves to chart the course.

By this time, things have clearly gotten out of hand as far as the Monetarists are concerned, and they disassociate themselves from anything further removed from the money supply than the monetary base.

Confused? Read on.

Some Helpful Hints

Where does all this leave someone who is trying to make an honest buck evaluating the posture of monetary policy? Instead of responding with a cliché (as is our custom)—such as "Life is tough for everyone"—we offer a series of helpful hints (HHs) to aid in interpreting Federal Reserve behavior.

1. Divide the indicators into two groups. One: *the monetary and reserve aggregates*—including the money supply (your favorite flavor), the monetary base, and total reserves. Two: *money market conditions*—especially interest rates on Treasury bills and the Federal funds rate.

2. Do not conclude that, because there has been an increase in the aggregates, monetary policy is embarked on a wild expansion. The money supply, for example, must increase with a growing economy in order to provide funds for the increased transactions associated with a larger GNP. The money supply has, in fact, increased in every year since 1950 save one (1957), although it can and has declined over shorter intervals (say three or six months).

3. Try to judge whether the aggregates, say the money supply, are growing faster than normal (expansionary policy) or slower than normal (restrictive policy). What is normal? The money supply grew at an annual rate of 4.0 percent during the twenty years from 1955 through 1975. From 1955 through 1965, however, its growth was only 2.2 percent a year, from 1966 through 1975 it was 5.9 percent, and from 1975 through 1979 the growth rate was 6.4 percent. Take your pick.

4. If interest rates are falling at the same time as the aggregates are increasing at a faster-than-normal rate, it is a good bet that the Federal Reserve has embarked on a course of monetary expansion. And if interest rates are rising at the same time as the aggregates are growing at a slower-than-normal rate, it is an equally good bet that the Federal Reserve has begun to exercise restraint.

5. The Federal Reserve publishes the minutes of the FOMC meetings with a thirty-day delay. Read them. If the Federal Reserve decided on increased monetary ease a month ago and your reading of the indicators shows it has not succeeded, look for signs of further easing as the Fed tries harder. If tighter monetary policy was decided upon a month ago and your reading of the indicators shows that the Federal Reserve hasn't succeeded—call your broker and sell.

Naturally, we assume no responsibility for the misfortunes brought down upon you when following these HHs. But we insist on 10 percent of the profits. For those of you who prefer to construct your own "super indicator" for monetary policy, you are invited to read the next chapter, which explains how to read the directive issued at the FOMC meetings and also treats you to a detailed look at the mechanics of open market operations.

READING 6

The Nuts and Bolts of Monetary Policy

At 11:15 in the morning of each business day, a long-distance conference call takes place among three men: Peter Sternlight, the manager of the System Open Market Account, who is located in the Federal Reserve Bank of New York; a member of the Board of Governors in Washington, D.C.; and a president of one of the other Federal Reserve banks currently serving on the Federal Open Market Committee. The job of the account manager is to carry out open market operations for the purpose of implementing the monetary policy directive issued at the last meeting of the FOMC. Each morning he reviews the operations planned for the day via the telephone hookup.

Although we have never listened in to what is said during one of these calls, we can make a pretty good guess at the conversation, much as sports commentators are able to surmise what is said at those all-important conferences between the quarterback and his coach in the closing minutes of a game, or the even more important huddle between a pitcher and catcher with men on second and third and none out. It probably goes something like this:

OPERATOR: San Francisco and Washington are standing by, New York. Will you deposit $3.35, please?

NEW YORK: You mean it's our turn to pay? Hold on a minute, operator, we don't seem to have enough change here.

61

WASHINGTON: This is Chairman Volcker on the line.

NEW YORK: Sorry, there's no one here by that name.

WASHINGTON: No, you don't seem to understand, I'm Chairman Paul Volcker and I want . . .

NEW YORK: Hello Paul, it's Peter. Sorry for the mix-up, but we've just hired a few Ph.D.s to man the phones, and they haven't gotten the hang of it quite yet.

WASHINGTON: I know just what you mean. Say, we've got a problem here. Our staff says the 6½ to 9 percent range for M1B should replace as the main target the 4 to 6½ percent range on M2. Or is it the other way around?

NEW YORK: Frankly, our people have urged me to look at the M3 numbers, trying to hit the fourth-quarter-to-fourth-quarter growth figures, rather than the two-month targets. They say the M1 ball game is over.

SAN FRANCISCO: Hello? Hello? When do we start?

If you think we have exaggerated the potential confusion confronting the Account Manager, a reading of some of the FOMC operating instructions should convince you otherwise. The primary thrust of monetary policy is summarized in the FOMC directive. Let's take a detailed look at how it is formulated and the ways in which it can be interpreted. We can then turn to the open market operations used in carrying it out.

The FOMC Directive

The Federal Open Market Committee meets about once every four weeks. At the beginning of each meeting, the staff of the FOMC, comprised of economists from the Board of Governors and the district Federal Reserve Banks, presents a review of recent economic and financial developments— what is happening to prices, unemployment, the balance of payments, interest rates, money supply, bank credit, and so on. Projections are also made for the months ahead. The meeting then proceeds to a discussion among the committee members; each expresses his views on the current economic and financial scene and proposes appropriate monetary policies.

The FOMC directive, embodying the committee's decision on the desired posture of monetary policy until the next meeting, is voted on toward the end of each meeting, with dissents recorded for posterity. If economic conditions are proceeding as had been expected and the current stance of monetary policy is still appropriate, the previous directive may remain unaltered. If conditions change, the directive is modified accordingly.

In recent years, the FOMC directive has usually contained five or six paragraphs. The first few review economic and financial developments, including the behavior of real output, inflation, monetary aggregates, and interest rates. The fourth or fifth paragraph then turns to a general qualitative statement of current policy goals. For example, at the meeting on February 6, 1979, the goals of the FOMC were set forth as follows:

> Taking account of past and prospective developments . . . it is the policy of the Federal Open Market Committee to foster monetary and financial conditions that will resist inflationary pressures while encouraging moderate economic expansion and contributing to a sustainable pattern of international transactions.

While the statement of goals does not contain everything —we know that the FOMC is not trying to eliminate environmental pollution (at least not yet)—it does include virtually every objective of stabilization policy. This general statement of goals is rarely changed significantly. Toward the end of 1975, for example, when in the throes of recession, the phrase "encouraging economic expansion" replaced "inflationary pressures" as the first goal mentioned.

Immediately following this general statement, the directive presents the long-run target ranges for the monetary aggregates that are thought to be consistent with the broadly stated goals. At the meeting of February 6, 1979, the annual targets were stated as follows:

> The Committee agreed that these objectives would be furthered by growth of M-1, M-2 and M-3 from the fourth quarter of 1978 to the fourth quarter of 1979 within ranges of 1½ to 4½ percent, 5 to 8 percent and 6 to 9 percent.

Two sources of flexibility appear in these annual targets. Obviously they can be changed each quarter. In our illustration, the growth rates are calculated from fourth-quarter 1978 to fourth-quarter 1979 but will then be altered to first-quarter 1979 through first-quarter 1980. Moreover, the ranges are rather broad, giving the Fed wide latitude in hitting the targets.

The last order of business in the FOMC directive is to specify the immediate requirements for the implementation of these longer-run objectives. In our by now familiar meeting of February 6, 1979, the specification was as follows:

> In the period before the next regular meeting, System open market operations are to be directed at maintaining the weekly average Federal funds rate at about the current level, provided that over the February-March period the annual rates of growth of M1 and M2, given approximately equal weight, appear to be within ranges of 3 to 7 percent and 5 to 9 percent, respectively.

Now we have a second set of monetary aggregate targets, this time specified for a two-month period. These two-month growth rates are altered, both to take into account "special events" as well as to be consistent with the longer-run objectives. Moreover, the Federal funds rate was used as still another short-run guideline, presumably to help the account manager hit the aggregate bull's eye. Unfortunately, during the past few years, the manager's accuracy leaves much to be desired. Perhaps there are too many numbers and too many targets floating around. It almost guarantees some confusion, as we suggested in our opening conversation.

Changed Emphasis in the Directive

The current emphasis in the directive is clearly on monetary aggregates. It wasn't always that way. In fact, until 1966 the directive to the account manager was couched solely in terms of money market conditions—easier or firmer. Free reserves and short-term interest rates ruled the day, especially the Treasury bill rate and the Federal funds rate.

In 1966, however, the directive was altered to include what was called a proviso clause. The account manager was directed, for example, "to conduct open market operations with a view towards somewhat firmer conditions in the money market, *provided* [our italics] that bank credit was not deviating significantly from projections." At the first meeting in 1970, the monetary aggregates in the directive were expanded to include money as well as bank credit in the proviso clause. At the third meeting in 1970, the monetary aggregates finally were put on a par with money market conditions. The committee expressed a desire to seek "moderate growth in money and bank credit over the months ahead" as well as "money market conditions consistent with that objective." Then, early in 1972, the FOMC added reserves as an operating target along with money market conditions.

Both money market conditions, especially the Federal funds rate, and reserves are supposed to help achieve a desired pattern of growth in monetary aggregates. Now that we know what must be done, let's see how they do it.

The Operating Room

Open market operations are performed in a well-guarded room within a fortresslike building in the heart of the nation's financial center. The Federal Reserve Bank of New York, designated by the FOMC as its operating arm, is located on Liberty Street only three blocks from Wall Street. This location permits Peter Sternlight, the manager of the Federal Reserve System Open Market Account, to be in close contact with the government securities dealers with whom the Federal Reserve System engages in purchases and sales of securities. Every morning of the workweek he meets with one or more of the securities dealers and gets the "feel of the market," as the opening handshakes (firm or limp? dry or sweaty palms?) telegraph whether the market is likely to be a tic tighter or easier. On occasion Sternlight has been known to shock the market by the judicious use of one of those little hand buzzers (the kind you used to be able to get in novelty shoppes).

Feedback from the securities dealers is only one component of the vast array of data and information marshaled by the account manager in mapping his plans for open market operations on any given day. The starting point, of course, is the directive issued by the FOMC at its last meeting. This expression of the proposed stance of monetary policy, together with the more precise range of desired movements in money market conditions and the monetary aggregates, provide the ultimate target for open market operations. Sternlight must still decide, however, how much to sell or buy, to or from whom, and when.

Money market conditions (particularly short-term interest rates) and monetary aggregates are directly affected by the reserves available to the banking system. Each workday morning, a little after 9:30, Sternlight receives a report on the reserve position of the banking system as of the night before. A sensitive indicator of pressure in this market is provided by the Federal funds rate.

A little later in the morning—but before the 11:15 conference call—the account manager is provided with a detailed projection by the research staff. It covers movements in various items that can affect the reserve position of the banking system—including currency holdings of the public, deposits in foreign accounts at the Federal Reserve Banks, and other technical factors. A change in any of these can cause reserves to go up or down and thereby affect bank lending capabilities, interest rates, and growth in the money supply. For example, as the public cashes checks in order to hold more currency, commercial banks must pay out vault cash and thereby suffer a loss in reserves. As foreign accounts at Federal Reserve banks increase—that is, as they present checks for payment drawn against commercial banks—reserves of commercial banks are transferred to foreign accounts at the Fed.

A call is also made to the U.S. Treasury to ascertain what is likely to happen to Treasury balances in tax and loan accounts at commercial banks—deposits of the U.S. government generated by tax payments of the public and receipts from bond sales—and to find out what is likely to happen to Treasury balances at the Federal Reserve Banks, from which most government expenditures are made. As funds are shifted from Treasury tax and loan accounts in commercial banks to Treasury balances at the Federal Reserve, the commercial banking system loses reserves.

By 11:00 A.M. Peter Sternlight has a good idea of money market conditions, including what is happening to interest rates, and of anticipated changes in the reserve position of the banking system. He also knows what the FOMC directive calls for. If the FOMC had asked for moderate growth in reserves in order to sustain moderate growth in the monetary aggregates, and all of the other factors just discussed are expected to pour a large volume of reserves into the banking system, he may decide that open market *sales* are necessary in order to prevent an excessive (more than moderate) expansion in reserves. If, on the other hand, he expects to find reserves going up too little or even declining as a result of these other forces, he may engage in significant open market purchases. It is now clear why knowledge that the Federal Reserve bought or sold so many or so few government securities on a given day or during a given week, in itself, tells us almost nothing about the overall posture or intent of monetary policy.

At the 11:15 conference call with a member of the Board of Governors in Washington and one of the Federal Reserve Bank presidents, Sternlight outlines his plan of action for the day and explains the reasons for his particular strategy. Once his decision is confirmed, the purchase or sale of securities (usually Treasury bills) takes place. The account manager instructs the traders in the trading room of the Federal Reserve Bank of New York to call the thirty-five or so government securities dealers and ask them for firm bids for stated amounts of specific maturities of government securities (in the case of a Fed open market sale) or for their selling price quotations for stated amounts of specific maturities (in the case of a Fed open market purchase). While the Federal Reserve does not engage in open market operations in order to make a profit, it still insists on getting the most for its money, and it is assured of that by vigorous competition among the various dealers in government securities.

It takes no more than thirty minutes for the trading desk to complete its "go-around" of the market and to execute the open market sale or purchase. By 12:30 the account manager and his staff are back to watching the situation and, if necessary, buying or selling additional amounts of government securities to implement the original objective.

Much is left to the judgment of the account manager, even with all of the double-checking with other parts of the Federal Reserve System. By and large, Peter Sternlight receives high marks for his job, despite the errors that inevitably enter any human undertaking. He is also a very pleasant fellow. There are some, however, who would have him, as well as (or especially) the FOMC, replaced by a computer, an automatic telephone, and a disembodied voice that periodically calls out orders to buy or sell $200, $300, or $400 million worth of government securities. The reasons for such an Orwellian prescription for the Federal Reserve are discussed in the next reading.

Fed Strategy: A Summary

Before ending this chapter let's pause a moment and survey the terrain. After so much on the intricacies of Fed policy making, the details have taken over and we are in danger, to coin a phrase, of losing the forest for the trees.

The ultimate purpose of the Federal Reserve is to influence total spending and GNP. But it has no way of directly altering GNP, so it has to exert its influence indirectly—through the supply of money and credit and various interest rates, mostly medium-term and long-term rates. However, these variables—let's call them the Fed's intermediate objectives—are not directly under the Fed's control either. So it has no choice but to aim at an *operating target,* perhaps several different ones, hoping that if it hits these operating targets they will eventually nudge the intermediate objectives and thereby get the job done.

This game plan is illustrated schematically in the accompanying chart. Notice the distinctions between operating targets, intermediate targets and ultimate objectives. Much of the confusion regarding Fed policy arises because these distinctions are ignored.

Notice also what is included in the concepts you will often encounter in the financial pages of your newspaper: the monetary aggregates, money market conditions, and the reserve aggregates.

The *monetary aggregates* are intermediate targets for the various measures M1A, M1B, M2, and M3. Other intermediate objectives are bank credit, total credit, and medium-term and long-term interest rates.

Money market conditions are one set of possible operating targets; the phrase refers to free reserves and money market interest rates—especially the Federal funds rate and to a lesser extent the three-month Treasury bill rate.

The *reserve aggregates* are another group of possible operating targets; the phrase includes a wide variety of bank reserve measures, such as the monetary base, total reserves, and so on. The chart above summarizes the arithmetic relationships among the various reserve measures. Interestingly,

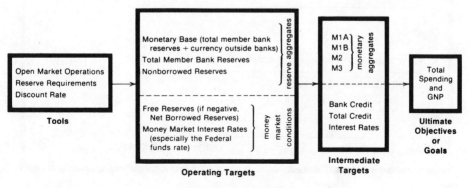

The Fed's Game Plan

the last of these—namely, free reserves—is usually considered an indicator of money market conditions rather than as one of the reserve aggregates.

In recent years, the Fed has been putting its plan into operation this way (more or less): It specifies its intermediate objective in terms of a desired range for monetary growth over the year—say an increase in M1B of from 5 to 8 percent. Then it sets an operating target for bank reserves that it figures will produce this rate of monetary growth—say an increase in total reserves or perhaps in nonborrowed reserves of from 4 to 6 percent over the year. Simultaneously, it sets another operating target—the Federal funds rate—that is thought to be consistent with the desired rate of increase in reserves.

The Federal funds rate has been used by the account manager as an indicator of the state of bank reserves. If reserves are growing too rapidly, the Federal funds rate will fall below target, signaling the account manager to intervene and drain reserves by open market sales. Alternatively, if reserves are growing too slowly, the Federal funds rate will rise above target, alerting the account manager to intervene and supply reserves by open market purchases.

This is the way it was until October 1979, when the Federal Reserve shifted its emphasis away from the Federal

---

MONETARY BASE (= total reserves + currency outside banks)
Minus Currency outside banks
_____

= TOTAL RESERVES

Minus member bank borrowing from the Fed
_____

= NONBORROWED RESERVES

Minus required reserves
_____

= FREE RESERVES (or, if negative, NET BORROWED RESERVES)

Relationships Among Alternative Reserve Measures

funds rate as an operating target, turning its attention to reserves instead. Whether this shift in favored operating targets is temporary or permanent is uncertain. And that cannot help but confuse matters for Fed-watchers.

Armed with these details, you can now return to the task of the last chapter: constructing an ideal indicator of Fed policy. If you come up with a winner, let us know.

READING 7

Should A Robot Replace the Federal Reserve?

Some Monetarists, most notably Milton Friedman, have abandoned countercyclical stabilization policy altogether. They never had any use for fiscal policy to begin with, and the issue of time lags in the impact of monetary policy has led them to jettison countercyclical monetary policy as well. Because of measurement difficulties, time lags make the implementation of monetary policy potentially hazardous.

"Countercyclical" monetary policy means leaning against the prevailing economic winds: easy money in recessions, to get the economy on the move again; tight money when there is a boom, to slow it down. In its most naive form, however, countercyclical monetary policy tends to ignore the complications bred by time lags.

Assume that the Federal Reserve forecasts a recession due six months from now. If the forecast is correct, and if a current expansion in the money supply would have an impact six months hence, well and good. But what if the Federal Reserve's crystal ball is not that clear, and it is more than a year before the main impact of today's monetary policy is reflected in the economy? Then the effects of today's expansionary monetary policy are likely to be felt *after* the economy has passed the trough and is already on its way up.

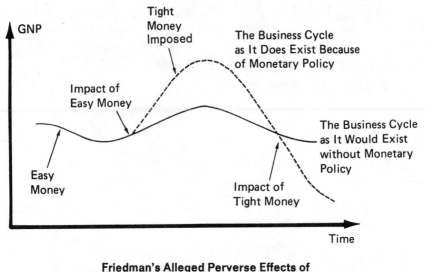

**Friedman's Alleged Perverse Effects of
Countercyclical Monetary Policy**

As the accompanying diagram illustrates, the impact of today's easy money may exacerbate tomorrow's inflation. This is Milton Friedman's explanation for the rampant inflation of 1969; the rapid rate of growth in the money supply in 1968, intended to forestall recession, lit the fuse of the inflationary time bomb that exploded the following year. Tight money will have similarly delayed effects; it may be imposed with the best of intentions, to curtail a boom, but its real impact, being long delayed, might accentuate a recession. And this occurred in its most reckless form in late 1974, so the argument goes. Excessively tight money was aimed at curtailing the rampant inflation; it precipitated the 1975 recession in the process. Monetary policy is a destabilizer rather than a stabilizer!

On these grounds—the precarious nature of economic forecasting and the alleged length, variability, and unpredictability of the time lags involved—Friedman and some other Monetarists have given up on orthodox monetary policy. Friedman argues that the economy has been and is now inherently stable, and that it would automatically tend to stay on a fairly straight course if only it were not being almost continuously knocked off the track by erratic or unwise monetary policies. Conclusion: quarantine the central bank. The best stabilization policy is no stabilization policy at all. Hasn't it all been said before:

> They also serve who only stand and wait.
>
> JOHN MILTON

Rules versus Discretion

What Professor Friedman proposes instead is that the Federal Reserve be instructed by Congress to follow a fixed long-run rule: Increase the money supply at a steady and inflexible rate, month in and month out, year in and year out, regardless of current economic conditions. Set the money supply on automatic pilot and then leave it alone.

The specific rule would depend on the definition of the money supply adopted. Actually, the particular number itself is not so important to Friedman as the restriction that once it is decided upon it be left alone thereafter. No tinkering!

The constant growth rule is intended to keep prices stable and employment high by allowing aggregate demand to grow secularly at the same rate as the growth in the economy's real productive capacity (due to growth in the labor force and increased productivity). It is also supposed to compensate, according to Friedman, for a long-term gradual downtrend in velocity—although, in fact, velocity has done nothing but rise since the end of World War II, and from all indications will continue to do so.

Such a rule, it is claimed, would eliminate forecasting and lag problems and therefore remove what Friedman sees as the major cause of instability in the economy—the capricious and unpredictable impact of countercyclical monetary policy. As long as the money supply grows at a constant rate each year, be it 3, 4, or 5 percent, any decline into recession will be temporary. The liquidity provided by a constantly growing money supply will cause aggregate demand to expand. Similarly, if the supply of money does not rise at a more than average rate, any inflationary increase in spending will burn itself out for lack of fuel. Anyway, any discretionary deviations by the central bank would interfere with the natural course of the economy and only make matters worse.

The United States Congress has been impressed enough to come part of the way toward a Friedman-type rule, in preference to allowing the Federal Reserve to rely entirely on its own judgment and discretion. In March 1975, both the House of Representatives and the Senate passed House Congressional Resolution 133, which instructed the Federal Reserve to "maintain long-run growth of the monetary and credit aggregates commensurate with the economy's long run potential to increase production." It also required that the Fed report quarterly to Congress on its target monetary and credit growth rates for the upcoming twelve months. In November 1977, these provisions were incorporated into the Federal Reserve Act itself.

The Friedman position is based on a number of pillars, each supported by mounds of statistical evidence produced by Friedmanites. However, very little is really known about the length and variability of the time lags. Such evidence as there is, and there is not much, is extremely mixed and inconclusive. Serious research on the subject is only in its early stages, and no consensus is apparent among economists who have worked in the area.

It is ironic—or instructive—that in the final analysis the extremists from both camps, Monetarist and Keynesian, have collectively ganged up on the Federal Reserve. The extreme Monetarists want to shackle it, because their concern with time lags leads them to believe it is both mischievous and harmful. The extreme Keynesians want to subordinate it to fiscal policy, because they think it is either useless or lethal.

In the middle, squabbling but finding more common cause than they had thought possible, are the moderates: moderate Monetarists, who believe that the forecasting-lag problem is not so great as to negate all the potential stabilizing effects of monetary policy; and moderate Keynesians, who believe that monetary policy probably does change interest rates and/or the availability of credit and that those changes, along with fiscal policy, probably do influence spending decisions in the right way at more or less the right time. While one group concentrates mainly on the money supply and the other primarily on credit conditions, they are nevertheless in agreement that some form of countercyclical monetary policy is necessary and, on balance, beneficial.

It seems clear, after all is said and done, that central banking is still at least as much art as science. We simply do not yet know enough to legislate an eternal rule, or even a rule for the next six months, that the Federal Reserve must follow under any and all circumstances. When we do know that much, the Federal Reserve will know it too, and if they are rational they will follow it regardless of whether it has been enacted into law.

Meanwhile, for better or worse, we appear to have no alternative but to rely on our best knowledge and judgment in the formulation of monetary policy. We can only try to make sure that the decision-makers are able and qualified people with open minds and the capacity to learn from experience.

READING 8

Fiscal Policy Versus Monetary Policy

The promoter of a match billed as Fiscal Policy versus Monetary Policy would surely be able to call this encounter the Main Event for the Heavyweight Title. Twenty-five years ago, however, such a contest would not have made even the preliminaries in the Featherweight division. A forfeit would have been declared in favor of fiscal policy. The reason? It was generally believed that monetary policy was unable to defend itself.

The dramatic resurgence of monetary policy since the 1950s rivals the most classic of comebacks. A quarter century ago, monetary policy was relegated to the subservient role of sweeper before the chariot of the Champion. Its functions were to keep bank reserves plentiful and the market for government securities firm, so that interest rates could remain low and nothing impede the right of way of the Great Man. Fiscal policy, alone, in all its glory, would promote full employment, stabilize prices, ensure economic growth, and eliminate poverty. The reader who thinks that this might be an exaggeration, which it probably is, should reread some of the more exuberant literature typical of that era.

Today they march to a different tune. Although some die-hard fans of fiscal policy still decry each move of the monetary authorities, calling every punch a foul and every feint unfair, their enthusiasm is not what it once was and their ranks have dwindled with the passage of time. Government economists now place monetary policy on an equal footing with fiscal policy in the pursuit of national economic objectives. Some academic economists even go so far as to argue that monetary policy should be *the* instrument of economic stabilization, that the impact of fiscal policy is negligible, at best. As we indicated earlier, much of the controversy centers about the debate between the Monetarists and the Keynesians.

How Fiscal Policy Works

According to the Monetarists, a change in the money supply will alter aggregate spending and GNP by a predictable amount, since the velocity of money is quite stable. Thus they contend that monetary policy is a much more effective instrument than fiscal policy.

Keynesians, on the other hand, are skeptical about the reliability of the relationship between the money supply and GNP. As they view it, a change in the money supply can alter aggregate spending only to the extent that it first changes interest rates or the availability of credit, and then only if business or household spending is sensitive to those changes. There is no direct link between the money supply and spending. Put briefly, the relationship between the money supply and GNP is seen as tenuous and variable, since fluctuations in the velocity of money may counteract changes in its supply.

In Keynesian eyes, changes in government spending or taxation—the primary tools of fiscal policy—*do* have a direct and fairly predictable impact on GNP. An increase in government spending raises GNP immediately. It also induces additional "multiplier effects" via a GNP-consumption-GNP link. As GNP rises because of an initial injection of government expenditure, consumers receive more income;

they spend a fraction of this increased income, which causes GNP to go up even further. For example, if government spending rises by $10 billion, income (or GNP) automatically goes up by $10 billion. Of this larger income, consumers will then spend a predictable fraction, say four-fifths, or $8 billion. Since spending by A is income to B, GNP goes up by this $8 billion as well. Of this, consumers then spend another four-fifths, or $6.4 billion. By now, GNP has gone up $24.4 billion. Eventually this process will come to a halt as the successive increments in income and spending become smaller and smaller; but the end result will be an increase in GNP by some multiple of the original increase in government spending.

Changes in tax rates are seen as having a similar multiple impact on GNP. If tax rates are lowered, consumers are left with more disposable income. They spend a predictable fraction of this, causing a rise in GNP, which in turn induces additional consumer expenditure. Conclusion: to bring about an expansion in spending and GNP, we should increase government spending and/or lower tax rates—that is, create a budget deficit. Anti-inflation policy would call for the opposite: reduce government spending and/or raise tax rates—that is, create a budget surplus.

It is important to note the central role of this GNP-consumption-GNP relationship in the Keynesian "multiplier" analysis. If consumer spending does not respond to changes in income, tax-rate changes would not affect spending or economic activity and the "multiplier effects" would be minimal.

Changes in government spending and/or tax rates can be implemented in many different ways. Government spending can be changed via military expenditures, outlays for education, urban renewal, farm price supports, medical research, the space program, or for any other specific government program. Tax receipts can be altered by changing the corporate income tax, the personal income tax, the investment tax credit, or any specific excise or sales tax.

How to Score (Old-Timers' Day)

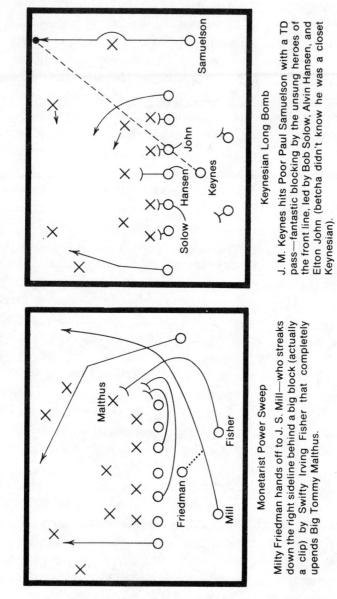

Monetarist Power Sweep

Milty Friedman hands off to J. S. Mill—who streaks down the right sideline behind a big block (actually a clip) by Swifty Irving Fisher that completely upends Big Tommy Malthus.

Keynesian Long Bomb

J. M. Keynes hits Poor Paul Samuelson with a TD pass—fantastic blocking by the unsung heroes of the front line, led by Bob Solow, Alvin Hansen, and Elton John (betcha didn't know he was a closet Keynesian).

While the impact of a change in any one of these tax or expenditure categories can be made virtually identical with a change in any other one, insofar as the arithmetic effect on GNP is concerned, profound social implications flow from which particular tax or expenditure program is or is not altered. For example, if we are experiencing substantial unemployment and a low rate of economic growth, and fiscal policy is decided upon as the appropriate remedy, a choice arises between lowering taxes and raising government spending. If we lower tax rates, the expansion in GNP will be brought about by private spending. On the other hand, if we increase government spending, this will give us more government services as well as more private purchases. Which alternative we choose should depend on the volume of government (social) services we want.

Going still further: if we decide that we should increase government spending, should it take the form of more money devoted to curbing environmental pollution or an expansion in urban renewal? When we are faced with inflationary pressures, should we cut back military expenditures or antipoverty programs? These issues involve social problems and policies that go far beyond the bounds of economics.

Measuring Fiscal Policy

Until now, we have discussed expansionary and contractionary fiscal policy in terms of deficits and surpluses in the federal budget. A budget deficit is expansionary and a budget surplus is contractionary. However, just as many widely used indicators of monetary policy are less than adequate (see Reading 5), so also are there serious limitations to using the *current* deficit or surplus as a guide to the stance of fiscal policy.

The measurement problem stems from the fact that tax receipts, and hence the size of the deficit or surplus, vary passively with GNP. Congress sets tax *rates,* not receipts; receipts then go up and down with GNP. Given the level of government spending, when GNP rises, tax receipts automatically increase and surpluses are automatically created (or deficits reduced). When GNP falls, tax receipts decline and deficits automatically result. Thus, it is impossible to draw any meaningful conclusions regarding the stance of fiscal policy by comparing a budget surplus in one year at one level of GNP, with a deficit in another year at a *different* level of GNP.

For example, the existence of a deficit during a recession suggests, at first glance, that fiscal policy is expansionary. It may be, however, that the tax structure is so steep that it drives income (and thereby tax receipts) down to recession levels. A deficit may thus actually be the result of a *contractionary* fiscal policy. The tax cut of 1964 was enacted primarily on the basis of such thinking; its intention was to reduce the "fiscal drag" on the economy. It was argued that the overly restrictive tax structure—with taxes rising too rapidly as GNP went up—made it virtually impossible for a rise in GNP to make any sustained headway.

The budget concept that *is* useful as an indicator of the posture of fiscal policy is called the full employment budget. The main problem in comparing deficits or surpluses in year X with year Y is that there are different levels of GNP in both years. As the diagram indicates, the idea of the full employment budget eliminates this problem by sticking to one concept of GNP, namely the full employment GNP. The full employment budget is defined as what the federal budget surplus (or deficit) *would be,* with the expected level of government spending and the existing tax structure, *if the economy were operating at the full employment level of GNP throughout the year.*

This calculated measure, the full employment budget, can be used to evaluate the effects and the performance of fiscal policy more meaningfully than the actual state of the budget, whatever it might be. Indeed, as an indicator of fiscal policy, the full employment budget is a much less ambiguous policy measure than any we thus far have been able to produce for monetary policy.

As an illustration, in 1962 GNP was well below its full employment potential. As the diagram indicates, a low level of GNP produces a poor tax harvest and, consequently, a deficit in the actual budget. Nevertheless, fiscal policy was hardly expansionary. In fact, it was quite the opposite; if GNP had been at the full employment level, or close to it, tax revenues would have risen so greatly that the *full employment budget* would have had a substantial surplus. Conclusion: the fundamental stance of fiscal policy was restrictive, not expansionary, and one reason for the high level of unemployment in 1962 stemmed from fiscal policy—even though the actual budget showed a deficit.

Thus, in a rare example of fiscal bravery, a tax cut was passed by Congress in 1964 despite the existence of a current budget deficit. A reduction in tax rates swings the tax receipts line (in the diagram) downward and diminishes the full employment surplus. An increase in government spending also shrinks the full employment surplus. A tax-rate

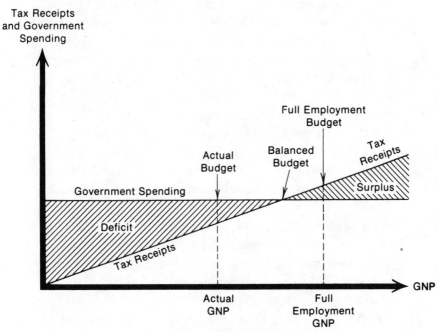

The Full Employment Budget

increase or a drop in government spending, both of which are restrictive actions, enlarge it. It is clear that changes in the full employment budget reflect basic *discretionary* changes in fiscal policy, as contrasted with movements in the actual budget that can be the *passive* result of fluctuations in GNP. In fact, an expansion in GNP due to a tax cut will succeed in lowering the size of the actual deficit.

All of this violates the most sacred canons of "traditional" (or pre-Keynesian) finance. According to the maxims of "orthodox" finance, an actual deficit is a signal to immediately set about balancing the budget by *raising* tax rates and/or *decreasing* government spending—this promptly drives GNP lower, thereby creating an even *larger* deficit, which makes matters worse all around.

Financial Aspects of Fiscal Policy

The fiscal policy mechanism described above is not the whole story. This is recognized by both Keynesians and Monetarists. The total impact on GNP of an expansionary fiscal policy cannot be fully ascertained until the method of financing government deficits is specified. Similarly, the net effect of a reduction in government spending and/or increases in tax rates cannot be fully calculated until the disposition of the surplus is taken into account.

When GNP goes up as the result of deficit spending, the public's need for day-to-day transactions money rises along with it. If the supply of money does not increase simultaneously, the public will find itself short of cash, will presumably sell off some financial assets in order to try to get additional money, and will thereby drive up interest rates. This so-called "crowding out" effect may inhibit private investment spending and home-building, partly offsetting the expansionary impact of the government's spending.

But a budget deficit can be financed in either of two ways. For one, the government might simply print money to finance itself. Since this is often frowned upon in the best of circles, its twentieth-century equivalent is used instead: the Federal Reserve buys the bonds that are sold by the government and in the process brand-new checking accounts are created for the government. If this is done, the increased supply of money will probably be sufficient to satisfy the enlarged need for money and interest rates will not rise. In this case, there will be little or no offset to the expansionary impact of the deficit spending, and GNP will be able to rise without interference from the monetary side.

Alternatively, the deficit might be financed by the sale of government securities to the public. If this is done, however, the pressure on financial markets is actually intensified, since the increase in the supply of new bonds on the market drives up the rate of interest even further. The sale of government securities will "crowd out" private borrowers, and the consequent decline in investment spending will offset an even larger portion of the increased government spending. The net effect, according to the Keynesians, is still expansionary, although less so than in the case of money-financed deficits.

In any event, regardless of details, the important point is that the execution of fiscal policy is inextricably mixed up with monetary implications. The two cannot be separated.

The Monetarists versus the Keynesians

The Keynesian position is that any fiscal action, no matter how it is financed, will have a significant impact on GNP. Keynesians do not deny that interest rates are likely to rise as GNP goes up, unless new money is forthcoming to meet cash needs for day-to-day transactions. Thus, they admit that a deficit financed by money creation is more expansionary than one financed by bond sales to the public, and that both are more expansionary than increased government spending financed by taxation. However, Keynesians do not believe that the decrease in private investment spending caused by higher interest rates (the "crowding out" effect) will be great enough to offset fully the government's fiscal actions. They think that the net impact on GNP will be significant, and in the right direction, regardless of what financing methods are used.

One reason for this conclusion is that higher interest rates are seen as having dual effects. They may reduce private investment spending, but they may also lead people to economize on their cash balances, thereby supplying part of the need for new transactions money from formerly idle cash holdings. Put somewhat differently, even if a deficit is not financed by new money, the velocity of existing money will accelerate (in response to higher interest rates) so that the old money supply combined with the new velocity will be able to support a higher level of spending and GNP.

The Monetarist view, on the other hand, is that unless a budget deficit is financed by new money creation it will not alter GNP. In order for GNP to rise, the money supply must expand. If a fiscal deficit is financed by printing money, it will indeed increase spending and GNP. But according to the Monetarists, it is not the deficit that is responsible—it is the additional money. Furthermore, a deficit is a very clumsy way to go about increasing the money supply. Why not simply have the Federal Reserve engage in open market operations? That would accomplish the same purpose, a change in the money supply, without getting involved in budget deficits or surpluses.

As the Monetarists see it, a fiscal deficit financed in any other way—as by selling bonds to the public—will not affect aggregate GNP. True, the government will be spending more. But others will wind up spending less. The "crowding out" effect is total and complete. Net result: no change in total spending or in GNP. The rise in government spending will *initially* increase GNP. However, this will increase the demand for cash for transactions purposes and drive interest rates up, and bond sales to finance the government's expenditures will drive rates up still further. The public will be buying government bonds and financing the government, instead of buying corporate bonds and financing business firms. The rise in interest rates will reduce private investment spending by as much as government spending is increased, and that will be the end of the story. Government fiscal policy, unaccompanied by changes in the supply of money, merely changes the proportion of government spending relative to private spending.

Anti-inflationary fiscal policy encounters similar objections from the Monetarists. An increase in tax rates that generates a fiscal surplus reduces private income and consumer spending. If the government destroys or simply holds the money, the tax revenues it has collected over and above its expenditures, then the surplus is accompanied by a reduction of the money supply in private pockets. Both Keynesians and Monetarists would agree that this is anti-inflationary, although for different reasons—the Keynesians because of the direct fiscal impact on consumer spending, with the tax increase reducing people's take-home pay, and the Monetarists because of the contraction in the money supply.

But if the government uses the surplus to retire part of the national debt, the funds flow back into the economy. The government retires debt by buying back its bonds. Bond prices are driven up, interest rates fall, and private investment spending increases. Keynesians would argue that GNP will still decline, that the debt retirement is a minor ripple on a huge wave. Monetarists, however, would say that private investment spending will increase until it replaces the cutback in consumer spending, leaving no net effect whatsoever on GNP.

In spite of these arguments, the confrontation between fiscal and monetary policy can be decided only by resort to empirical evidence. The Keynesians claim that the power of fiscal policy was demonstrated by the success of the 1964 tax cut in bringing the economy up to a high level of employment. The Monetarists contend that fiscal policy alone is useless and that it was the rapid expansion of the money supply during the months preceding the tax cut that did the job. They also point to the failure of the 1968 tax surcharge to stop inflation. The Keynesians respond by asserting that acceleration of the war in Vietnam undid the impact of the 1968 tax increase.

Frustrated, let us turn to Federal Reserve's model for a decision. The accompanying figure shows the simulated response in nominal GNP (left side) and real GNP (right side) to a $10 billion expansion in government expenditure. In each of the pictures there are three lines, each representing alternative monetary policies accompanying the expansionary fiscal policy. The solid line shows the effect with a monetary policy that keeps the three-month Treasury bill rate unchanged. That assumption implies an expansion in the money stock to accommodate rising demand as GNP goes up. The dotted line assumes a monetary policy that keeps bank reserves (but not necessarily the money supply) unchanged. The dot-dash line simulates the results with a constant money stock.

It is evident from the pictures that this last monetary policy causes a substantial amount of crowding out, as we would expect. The fixed money stock policy forces rates of interest to rise as GNP increases and this cuts off investment spending. Note, however, that there isn't complete crowding out of nominal GNP, although in the right-hand picture there is complete crowding out of real GNP after about two years.

The multiplier effects of government spending are much more expansionary with the two more accommodating monetary policies. Thus the Fed model confirms the crucial role of money for the size of the fiscal policy multipliers. But the Fed model maintains that complete crowding out does not take place even with a fixed money stock assumption.

The Monetarist model of the Federal Reserve Bank of St. Louis is less wishy-washy than its sparring partner: An increase of $1 billion in the money supply raises GNP by over $5 billion after one year, while a similar increase in government spending has *zero* impact on GNP over the same time period. An increase in government spending raises GNP after six months, but by the time a year has elapsed, other types of spending have been crowded out to offset the expan-

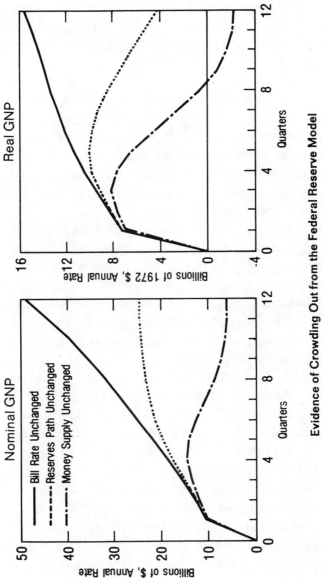

Evidence of Crowding Out from the Federal Reserve Model

sion in government expenditures. What other types of spending? On this the St. Louis model is silent, just as it is silent on the transmission mechanism through which money affects spending. Indeed, it is this agnosticism on the transmission process and the surprising result with respect to fiscal policy that make the St. Louis model incomprehensible to many Keynesians.

Who gets the verdict has implications far beyond flattering the egos of economists with vested intellectual interests on opposite sides of the fence. If we are in a recession and use easy money to raise GNP, interest rates will fall and private investment and home-building will expand. On the other hand, if we use fiscal policy—lowering tax rates or increasing government spending—consumer spending or social services will be favored instead.

If we are in a boom and want to reduce aggregate spending, tight money will hit housing hard; tight fiscal policy probably will not. If a vibrant housing industry is important for national social and economic welfare—on the theory that the American Dream consists of each citizen owning his own house with a well in the backyard—perhaps we should rely mainly on easy money to stop recessions and mainly on tight fiscal policy to halt inflation.

A rational overall stabilization policy would evaluate all of these elements, and more, before embarking on a course of action. There are likely to be other side effects, some desirable, others undesirable. Often political considerations will be involved as well. It is difficult, for example, to raise taxes in an election year. Not to mention the influence that various pressure groups, both business and labor, are likely to bring to bear on such decisions.

In any case, the importance of *both* fiscal and monetary policy, and the numerous interrelations between them, make it plain that there can be no clear-cut winner. If either fiscal policy or monetary policy is declared the victor, to the neglect and subjugation of the other, it is we who will be the losers.

READING 9

Should We Worry about the National Debt?

"Personally," said President Eisenhower, in his State of the Union Message in 1960, "I do not feel that any amount can properly be called a surplus as long as the nation is in debt. I prefer to think of such an item as a reduction in our children's inherited mortgage."

In the same vein, Senator Harry F. Byrd, Sr. pondered the $275 billion national debt in 1955 and gloomily predicted: "The debt today is the debt incurred by this generation, but tomorrow it will be debt on our children and grandchildren, and it will be for them to pay, both principal and interest."

Debt worriers are fond of statistical computations. We now have a national debt of some $800 billion (in the form of marketable and nonmarketable government securities, held by the public and by government agencies) and a population of about 220 million. Conclusion: every man, woman, and child in this country owes about $3,635 whether he knows it or not. Every newborn infant starts life not only with a pat on the back but also with a $3,635 share of the national debt hanging over his or her head.

Agonizing over the size of the public debt is one of our major national preoccupations. Is the situation really all that bad? Are the debt worriers right when they warn us that, by passing on a national debt of $800 billion, we are burdening future generations with a weight that will be almost impossible for them to bear? Are they correct in cautioning us, with stern voices, that we are penalizing those as yet unborn by forcing them to pay for our own vices and follies?

The National Debt Equals the National Credit

The national debt is essentially the net result of past and present fiscal policy, mostly past. It is the sum of all past deficits, less surpluses, in the federal budget. A budget deficit requires that the government either print money or borrow to cover the deficit, and most modern governments choose to borrow (that is, sell government securities). As a result, we acquire a national debt, embodied in the form of government bonds; the total of government securities outstanding *is* the national debt. It is increased by every additional deficit we incur and finance by issuing more bonds.

If the national debt is a debt, we must owe it to someone. Indeed we do—we owe it mostly to ourselves. Most of our government's bonds are internally held, that is, they are owned by citizens of the United States. Thus, while we the people (as the United States) *owe* $800 billion, we the people (as owners of government securities) are simultaneously *owed* close to the same amount. A government bond is, after all, an asset for whoever buys it.

All evidences of debt must appear on *two* balance sheets, and government securities are no different from any other IOU in this respect. Every IOU appears on the balance sheet of the debtor, as a liability; but it also turns up, not surprisingly, on the balance sheet of whoever is holding it, its owner, this time as an *asset.* Thus, every liability necessarily implies the existence of a financial asset owned by someone else. For the same reason, every *financial* asset implies a corresponding liability on the part of someone else.

This accounting gem has interesting ramifications. It means, for one, that merely creating money cannot, in and of itself, make a country richer, a conclusion that always pleases conservatives. After all, money is a financial asset, which implies that somewhere else there is a corresponding liability. If liabilities go up as rapidly as assets, the country as a whole (including both the government and the private sector) can be getting no richer.

Most of our money is in the form of demand deposits, which are liabilities of banks. The part of our money that is in the form of coin or currency is a liability of either the United States Treasury or the Federal Reserve, depending on which agency issued it.

Thus merely creating money can hardly make a nation richer, no matter how much it creates. To become richer—to increase its net worth—a country must increase its output of *real* assets, its production of real goods and services. As conservatives like to point out, if we want to become wealthier, we must work harder and produce more. Printing money, per se, will not do it.

By the same token, however, exactly the same logic also implies that another favorite conservative incantation is equally false: namely, the belief that increasing the national debt makes a country poorer. Government bonds are liabilities of the government but are financial assets to whoever owns them. If the national debt increases, someone's financial assets go up as much as the government's liabilities. If domestically held assets rise along with liabilities, the country as a whole can be getting no poorer.

The very term *national debt* is thus a half-truth. If it is a domestically held debt, it could just as well be called the *national credit*. Both labels are half-truths. As with all liabilities, it is *both* a debt (to the borrower) *and* a credit (to the lender).

To become poorer—to reduce its net worth—a country must reduce its holdings of real assets, curtail its production of *real* goods and services. Increasing the national debt, no matter how high, cannot in and of itself make a country poorer so long as it is owned internally. (Actually, about $125 billion of our $800 billion national debt is held by foreign citizens and institutions.)

Nor does an increasing national debt, just because of its size, impose a burden on future generations. As long as the debt is held internally, neither the interest nor the principal represents a dead weight on the backs of our children and grandchildren. The taxes that must be raised to pay the interest are merely transfers from one group within the economy, the taxpayers, to another group, the bondholders. Future generations inherit tax liabilities, but they also inherit bonds and the right to receive the interest on them.

Even if the debt had to be paid off, future generations, as inheritors of the bonds, would be making payments of the principal to themselves. In fact, of course, the federal debt never has to be fully repaid any more than does the debt of any going concern, public or private. As parts of the debt come due, they can be repaid with fresh borrowings. Continuous refinancing is typical of the modern successful corporation, because confidence in the company's ability to earn future income makes holding its bonds both safe and profitable. Similarly, confidence in the continuing viability and taxing power of the federal government eliminates the need for net repayment of principal, either currently or in the future.

The Real Burden of the Debt: I

Does this mean, then, that the debt worriers are completely off the track? Not quite, and therein lies the story of the *real* burden of the debt as contrasted with the imaginary burden.

In the first place, holdings of government bonds are not evenly distributed among the population. Some of us have more than our $3,635 share, much more; and some have less, much less. Thus current interest payments on the debt, while "only" an internal transfer from taxpayers to bondholders, may create problems of legitimate concern to the public. If taxpayers are largely from the lower and middle income groups, while bondholders are primarily in the upper income brackets, then the tax collection → interest payment transfer will increase the inequality of income distribution. Little is known about the pattern of interest payments on the government debt according to income of the recipient. This transfer *may*, therefore, interfere with social objectives of reducing income inequality.

Furthermore, if the federal debt grows at a faster rate than GNP, tax rates may have to be increased in order to meet interest payments. Higher tax rates may reduce work incentives. If so, production falls and overall economic well-being decreases. In the United States, however, the national debt has actually declined, quite substantially, as a proportion of our gross national product. In 1945, the national debt was about 130 percent of GNP; in 1955, 70 percent; in 1965, 45 percent; and in 1979 it was 35 percent.

Even if the debt falls as a proportion of GNP, if interest *rates* go up sufficiently then tax rates may have to be raised to meet the interest payments, thus again possibly reducing work incentives. Interest rates have indeed risen since 1945, but nevertheless the interest "burden"—interest charges as a proportion of GNP—has not increased. Over the past thirty years, annual interest payments have been stable at between 1½ and 2½ percent of GNP, with the most recent figure hovering at 2 percent.

The Real Burden of the Debt: II

Aside from the possible income-redistribution and work-incentive problems associated with interest payments on the national debt, there is one way in which the debt might impose a burden, a cost, on future generations. This involves not the interest, but the principal itself.

As we noted above, a country will become poorer only if it reduces its output of real assets, its ability to produce real goods and services. In this very meaningful sense the wealth of future generations can be measured by the real capital stock they inherit, the real productive capacity of the economy we bequeath to them. A smaller capital stock permits less production, hence less consumption. A larger capital stock enables the economy to produce more, hence consume more.

Assume that the economy is already operating at a full capacity rate of production and that the budget is balanced. Whereupon the government increases its spending, financing its additional expenditures by sufficient new *taxation* to forestall inflation. In this case, the increased use of resources by the government comes primarily at the expense of consumption. Consumers, left with less after-tax income, have to cut back their spending by as much as government spending has been stepped up.

Alternatively, under the same initial circumstances, assume that the additional government spending is *debt-financed* rather than tax-financed, and that a tight monetary policy is used along with debt-financing to prevent inflation. Now interest rates will rise and the increased use of resources by the government will come primarily at the expense of investment instead of consumption. The higher interest rates will release resources from private investment for use by the government, with investment spending cut back by as much as government spending has been increased.

As a result, the production of new plant and equipment will be curtailed, and future generations will consequently inherit a smaller capital stock. Future productive capacity is lower than it might have been. In this limited sense, the "burden" of debt-financed current government expenditure is transferred to future generations.

Two qualifications are necessary. First, note that the argument assumes we start from a full capacity rate of production, roughly a full employment level of GNP. If the additional government spending were to take place during a recession, when there are idle resources available, then there would be no "burden" on future generations, no matter how it was financed. During a recession there are unemployed resources that can be tapped, so the government can increase its spending without anyone else reducing theirs. There would be no reason to permit a rise in interest rates, since the danger of inflation would be minimal, and an expansion in spending and GNP would be beneficial to all.

Under such circumstances, the future capital stock is not diminished. In fact, if the government's deficit spending succeeds in getting us out of the recession, the future capital stock will probably be *enlarged.* Thus increasing the national debt during a recession, instead of imposing a burden on future generations, is actually doing them a favor.

Second, the "burden" argument totally ignores what the government spends the money on. Assuming full employment, if the government's expenditure is for current consumption purposes—such as subsidizing inexpensive lunches for Congressmen or schoolchildren—then total capital passed on to the future is indeed reduced. But if the government builds highways or dams, or increases any type of capital asset that raises future productivity, the increased investment by the government replaces the decreased investment by private business. Future generations will inherit the same capital stock, except more will be in the form of public capital and less in the form of private capital.

Moving from theory to reality, the fact of the matter is that a significant part of our public debt stems directly from World War II military spending. In 1941 our national debt was $65 billion, and in 1945 it was $280 billion. Most of these expenditures occurred during a period of full employment. Yet few would call this a burden passed on to the future. Without it, we might well have had no future.

The Nuts and Bolts of Debt Management

Given a national debt of $800 billion, its day-to-day management has implications for the functioning of financial markets and for economic stability. How can the debt be refinanced most smoothly when portions of it come due? How much of the debt should be in the form of short-term Treasury bills, how much in the form of long-term Treasury bonds?

The dimensions of the Treasury's debt-management chore can best be appreciated by realizing that about $230 billion of the debt comes due every year and must be paid off. How? By refinancing it, of course—that is, by borrowing $230 billion from someone else. The Treasury can replace the maturing issues with new short-term Treasury bills, or with intermediate- or long-term bonds, thus providing some elbow room for altering the maturity structure of the debt.

What are the objectives of day-to-day debt management? One goal is to minimize the interest cost of the debt to the taxpayers. But this can hardly be the only objective. If it were, the Treasury could minimize the interest cost—indeed, reduce it to zero—by simply printing money and buying back all the outstanding securities. That is, it could replace its interest-bearing debt (bills and bonds) with its noninterest-bearing debt (money). Obviously, the Treasury does not "monetize the debt," because to do so would probably result in massive inflation, and the Treasury also has the objective of managing the debt to promote economic stability.

These two objectives often dictate opposite policy actions. Minimizing the interest cost suggests that when we are in a recession, and interest rates are low across the board, the Treasury should refund its maturing issues with new long-term bonds, thus ensuring low interest payments for itself well into the future. During boom periods, on the other hand, when interest rates are typically high, the Treasury should refinance by selling short-term issues, Treasury bills, so the government does not have to continue paying high rates after yields have fallen to more normal levels.

Stabilization objectives call for just the opposite policies. When we are in a recession, the last thing we want to do is to raise long-term interest rates, which is precisely what pushing long-term securities onto the market is likely to accomplish. Boom periods, when we *do* want to raise long rates, are when we should sell long-term bonds.

Thus the objective of minimizing interest costs dictates lengthening the maturity structure of the debt (more long-term bonds relative to short-term bills) during recession periods and shortening the maturity structure during boom periods. For purposes of economic stabilization we should do the opposite—try to shorten the maturity structure during recessions and lengthen it during prosperity.

A complication that makes it difficult to lengthen the maturity structure of the federal debt is the archaic 4¼ percent legal ceiling on government bond interest rates. By virtue of a law passed in 1917, the Treasury is not allowed to pay more than a 4¼ percent interest rate on bonds with seven or more years to maturity. Since long-term market interest rates have generally been well above 4¼ percent in recent years, the Treasury has been unable to offer competitive yields on long-term securities and thus has had no choice but to borrow via shorter-maturity issues. (In a daring break with tradition, Congress grabbed the bull by the tail and faced the situation squarely; it modified the law and permitted the Treasury to issue up to $27 billion of bonds at rates above 4¼ percent.)

Debt-management policy must be administered in coordination with monetary and fiscal policy. If minimizing the interest cost is the primary goal of the Treasury, then monetary and fiscal policy will have to take appropriate action to offset this counterstabilization debt policy. If economic stabilization is the primary objective of debt management, then the monetary and fiscal authorities can take this into account and reduce the forcefulness of their own actions.

Coordination between the monetary and debt-management authorities is also essential on a continuing basis because of the vast magnitude of the Treasury's frequent refunding operations. When the Treasury refinances a large volume of maturing issues and decides to replace them with longer-term issues, it often needs help from the central bank. If the Federal Reserve is pursuing a tight money policy, for example, it will often become less aggressive and resort to a policy of keeping an "even keel" in the bond markets as the date of a refinancing approaches. In effect, the central bank will mark time for a few weeks while the Treasury goes through the mechanics of the refunding operation. It is difficult enough for the Treasury to roll over so much debt without being forced to cope with additional complications resulting from actions of the monetary authorities.

Monetary policy, fiscal policy, and debt management are often considered the three primary tools of stabilization policy. In practice, however, debt management has typically been the runt of the litter. Perhaps that is just as well. Given the power of monetary and fiscal policy to implement national economic goals, perhaps debt management can make its most significant contribution by successfully accomplishing the more limited but not unimportant task of continuously refinancing a very large volume of government securities without unduly disturbing the nation's financial markets.

Inflation:—How to Gain and Lose at the Same Time

We had sold out almost our entire inventory and, to our amazement, had nothing to show for it except a worthless bank account and a few suitcases full of currency not even good enough to paper our walls with. We tried at first to sell and then buy again as quickly as possible—but the inflation easily overtook us. The lag before we got paid was too long; while we waited, the value of money fell so fast that even our most profitable sale turned into a loss. Only after we began to pay with promissory notes could we maintain our position. Even so, we are making no real profit now, but at least we can live. Since every enterprise in Germany is financed in this fashion, the Reischsbank naturally has to keep on printing unsecured currency and so the mark falls faster and faster. The government apparently doesn't care; all it loses in this way is the national debt. Those who are ruined are the people who cannot pay with notes, the people who have property they are forced to sell, small shopkeepers, day laborers, people with small incomes who see their private savings and their bank accounts melting away, and government officials and employees who have to survive on salaries that no longer allow them to buy so much as a new pair of shoes. The ones who profit are the exchange kings, the profiteers, the foreigners who buy what they like with a few dollars, kronen, or zlotys, and the big entrepreneurs, the manufacturers, and the speculators on the exchange whose property and stocks increase

103

without limit. For them practically everything is free. It is the great sellout of thrift, honest effort, and respectability. The vultures flock from all sides, and the only ones who come out on top are those who accumulate debts. The debts disappear of themselves.[1]

Inflation is considered by most people as equal to or second only to unemployment among the nation's major aggregate economic problems. In almost every presidential campaign, candidates call inflation a bad thing and vow to control it once elected. The rising cost of groceries, auto repairs, medical services, clothes, travel, and everything else is a main topic of conversation among consumers. Business firms realize that higher prices for materials, labor, equipment, and other things they buy will reduce business profits unless they are successful in passing these higher costs on to the consumer in the form of higher consumer prices. Inflation is a prime bargaining consideration in labor union negotiations. A stated national goal of government economic policy is to stabilize the price level. All groups comprising the population—consumers, unions, business firms, and government—are concerned about inflation.

MEANING AND MEASUREMENT OF INFLATION

Most people have a good idea of what is meant by inflation. They know that it causes a sack full of groceries to cost more money. They know that buying Christmas presents costs more. They know that it is more expensive to eat out, to go to a movie, to take a vacation, or to buy a car. They know they will be generally worse off in the future unless their pay can keep up with inflation.

Inflation defined

Inflation means that the general level of prices is rising. That is, enough commodity prices are rising so that, on the average, prices in general are rising. During inflation some commodities may be falling in price and some may be rising, but the commodities rising in price are dominant, and they exert an upward force on the general price level.

Further aspects of inflation

Dynamic aspects. An aspect of inflation that needs to be stressed is its dynamic and self-sustaining properties. Increases in the price level

---

[1]Erich Maria Remarque, *The Black Obelisk* (New York: Harcourt, Brace and Co., 1957), pp. 54–55.

induce economic groups to react to rising prices, causing further in- *feeds on* creases in prices. For example, consumers expecting increases in *its* prices may increase current consumer spending, causing current mar- *own* ket prices to rise. During periods of rising prices, producers are not *velocity* inclined to resist increases in wages and other costs, since higher pro- duction costs may be shifted forward to consumers in the form of higher prices. These increases in prices, however, become the basis for further increases in production costs and still higher prices.

Inflation without rising prices. Inflation is not always observable in the form of rising prices. It may be suppressed; market prices may not reflect the inflationary forces operating in the economy. *Suppressed inflation* is usually associated with an attempt on the part of the government to control prices. For example, the government decreed a 90-day price freeze period beginning August 15, 1971. During the freeze period prices remained about the same. Inflationary forces, however, continued to exist. The reason is that the government did not do anything to alter the relationship of demand and supply. Inflation existed in the economy because aggregate output demanded exceeded aggregate output supplied at existing market prices.

Measurement of inflation

Inflation is measured by price index numbers. Price index numbers indicate the general level of prices in reference to a base year. For example, the consumer price index in 1977 was 181.5, using 1967 as the base year. This means that prices on the average were 81.5 percent above prices in 1967. The consumer price index increased further, to 195.3, in 1978. What was the rate of inflation between 1977 and 1978? The answer is 7.6 percent. This was derived as follows:

$$\text{Rate of inflation} = \frac{195.3 - 181.5}{181.5} = 7.6\%$$

Consumer and wholesale price indices. Table 10–1 shows the behavior of consumer and wholesale prices between 1929 and 1978. The U.S. Bureau of Labor Statistics computes both these series of price indices. The consumer price index, sometimes referred to as the cost-of-living index, includes commodities which city wage earners and clerical workers buy, such as food, housing, utilities, transportation, clothing, health, and recreation. The wholesale price index includes hundreds of commodities such as farm products and processed foods, as well as industrial commodities such as textiles, fuels, chemicals, rubber, lumber, paper, metals, machinery, furniture, nonmetallic minerals, and transportation equipment.

TABLE 10–1
Consumer price index and wholesale price
index in selected years, 1929–1978
(1967 = 100)

Year	Consumer price index	Wholesale price index
1929.........	51.3	49.1
1940.........	42.0	40.5
1950.........	72.1	81.8
1960.........	88.7	94.9
1962.........	90.6	94.8
1964.........	92.9	94.7
1966.........	97.2	99.8
1968.........	104.2	102.5
1970.........	116.3	110.4
1971.........	121.3	113.9
1972.........	125.3	119.1
1973.........	133.1	134.7
1974.........	147.7	160.1
1975.........	161.2	174.9
1976.........	170.4	182.9
1977.........	181.5	194.2
1978.........	195.3	209.3

Source: *Economic Report of the President,
January 1977*, pp. 242, 247; *Monthly Labor Review*, May 1979, p. 85; *Business Conditions Digest*, February 1979, p. 87.

Construction of a price index. Since inflation is measured by price index numbers, it is important to understand how price index numbers are derived. A simple illustration can point out the essential principles underlying their construction. Suppose a family spends $10,000, $10,500, and $11,000 in 1975, 1976, and 1977, respectively, for identical baskets of goods. If 1975 is used as the base year, the index number for the goods for that year is 100. It is 105 for 1976, calculated by dividing the cost of the basket in the base year ($10,000) into the cost in 1976 ($10,500) and multiplying by 100 in order to remove the decimal. Using the same procedure, the index number in 1977 is 110, or

$$\frac{\text{Cost of market basket (1977)}}{\text{Cost of market basket (1975)}} \times 100 = \frac{\$11,000}{\$10,000} \times 100 = 110$$

The basket of goods used to compute price index numbers is a representative sample. The quantities of each good in the basket—the number of dresses, shirts, loaves of bread, gallons of gasoline, movie tickets, television sets, autos, and so forth—bought during the year are specified. The sum of the price times the quantity of each good in the basket gives the value of the basket. After the value of the basket is calculated, the final step in the construction of a price index is to select the base year and compute the index numbers as illustrated.

A set of price index numbers is not a perfect measure of inflation. Only a sample of commodities is included in the index. What constitutes a representative sample is difficult to determine, and it changes over time in response to changes in tastes and preferences of people. It is also difficult to account for changes in the quality of goods that occur over time; for some goods and services, higher index numbers reflect higher costs for a better commodity rather than higher cost for the same commodity. Despite these imperfections, price index numbers are still useful indicators of trends in the level of prices.

ECONOMIC EFFECTS OF INFLATION

Inflation affects the distribution of income, the allocation of resources, and the national output. The effects of inflation on the distribution of income are referred to as the *equity* effects, and its effects on resource allocation and national output are called the *efficiency* and *output* effects of inflation, respectively.

Equity effects

The impact of inflation is uneven. Some people benefit, and some are worse off due to inflation. Because inflation alters the distribution of income, a major concern is the degree of equity or fairness in the distribution of income.

Anyone who is on a fixed income is hurt by inflation, since it reduces real income. For example, a person who earns $10,000 a year during an inflationary period in which there is a 25 percent increase in the price level suffers a cut in real income equivalent to the rate of inflation—$2,500 in this illustration. Examples of those whose incomes often do not rise as fast as the price level are retired persons on pensions, white-collar workers, civil servants, persons on public assistance, and workers in declining industries.

People who hold assets in the form of money and who have fixed claims on money may be worse off by inflation. Suppose a person deposits $1,000 in a savings account and receives a 5 percent interest rate, or $50 during the year. If the rate of inflation is in excess of 5 percent, the real value of the original savings of $1,000 plus the $50 earned on the savings for a year is reduced to less than the original $1,000. Creditors and owners of mortgages and life insurance policies are hurt by inflation, since the real value of their fixed money claims is reduced. People who bought government savings bonds for $18.75 and were paid $25.00 at maturity ten years later have sometimes discovered that the $25.00 would not buy the same quantity of goods and services as the $18.75 would have bought ten years earlier.

Inflation benefits people who have incomes that rise faster than prices and those who hold assets whose values rise faster than the price level. Wages and salaries of workers in rapidly growing industries are likely to rise faster than the price level. Teachers' salaries grew faster than the price level during the 1960s; therefore, teachers enjoyed absolute and relative real income gains during the period, due to the relative expansion in the demand for education. Strong unions are sometimes successful in bargaining for wage increases that are greater than the increases in the price level. People who depend upon income in the form of profits—owners of stocks and business enterprises—may have increases in real income, depending upon the rate of increase in profits in comparison to prices. The value of land and improvements on land may rise during inflation; if they rise in value faster than the rate of inflation, owners of property will benefit.

In summary, inflation alters the distribution of income and wealth.[2] Inflation is like a tax to some people and like a subsidy to others. Persons whose real incomes are reduced by inflation are those who have fixed incomes and hold assets in the form of money. Persons whose real incomes are increased by inflation are those who have money income that increases faster than prices and hold real assets that appreciate in value faster than inflation. The arbitrary manner in which inflation may change the pattern of income distribution gives support to the claim that inflation is inequitable.

Efficiency effects

Inflation tends to change the pattern of resource allocation. In a competitive market the prices of different goods and services reflect differences in consumer valuations of the quantities made available. Inflation causes demands for different goods and services to increase, but demands for some increase more rapidly than those for others. Increases in demands evoke supply responses, the extent of which varies from product to product. Thus inflation changes relative demands, relative supplies, and relative prices of different goods and services. The pattern of resource allocation, then, is not the same pattern that would exist in the absence of inflation. It is not certain that

---

[2]It is assumed that inflation is unanticipated. A fully anticipated inflation may not alter the distribution of income and wealth.

the pattern of resource allocation with inflation is less efficient (that is, results in lower economic welfare) than the pattern without inflation.[3] However, many economists argue that inflation distorts the pattern of resource allocation, implying a less efficient pattern when inflation occurs.

Inflation encourages economic groups to spend time and resources in an attempt to adjust to inflation. For an example, since inflation reduces the purchasing power of money, it encourages everyone to economize or minimize their money balances, that is, assets which are held in the form of money. The time spent and the resources used in adjusting to inflation could have been used to produce goods and services. Thus, inflation, by encouraging everyone to make adjustments and divert time and resources away from production, reduces economic efficiency.

Output effects

The preceding discussion of the equity and efficiency effects of inflation was presented on the assumption of levels of real output and production that lie on the economy's production possibilities curve. This was done in order to focus attention on how inflation may alter the distribution of real income among people (equity effects) and the allocation of resources (efficiency effects). To state this simply, a certain size pie was assumed in the previous discussion, and the concern was how inflation altered the slices of pie and how inflation affected the use of resources in making the pie. Now we consider what the effects of inflation are on the size of the pie. What are the effects of inflation on the level of output of goods and services?

Inflation may have a stimulating effect on production and employment in the economy. The argument in support of this proposition can be presented as follows: During inflation money wages lag behind price increases. Thus, real profit income is increased. Under the stimulus of higher profits, producers expand production and employ more people.

The argument that inflation may stimulate production and employment should be qualified. Runaway or hyperinflation may depreciate the value of money so drastically that it loses its acceptability as a medium of exchange. Under these circumstances a barter economy develops, accompanied by lower production levels and higher unemployment. If the economy is operating at full capacity and full employ-

---

[3]Frank G. Steindl, "Money Illusion, Price Determinancy and Price Stability," *Nebraska Journal of Economics and Business,* no. 10 (Winter 1971), pp. 26–27.

ment, then, of course, inflation cannot stimulate them further. Inflation at full employment is referred to usually as *pure* inflation.

The impact of inflation differs depending upon whether or not inflation is associated with increases in production and employment. As long as production is rising, there is a check on inflation since, although lagging behind demand, supply is increasing, thus tending to mitigate inflationary forces. Also, the equity effects of inflation are minimized if production and employment are rising. However, as the economy approaches full employment, the seriousness of inflation increases. The possibility of an accelerated rate of inflation is nearer, and the possible beneficial effects of inflation on production and employment are remote.

ROLE OF MONEY IN THE INFLATIONARY PROCESS

It is important to understand the role of money in the inflationary process. After a discussion of the meaning and functions of money, we shall discuss the significance of money as an economic variable. This discussion centers around a development of the so-called equation of exchange and the quantity theory of money.

Meaning and functions of money

Money serves three basic functions: a medium of exchange, a measure of value, and a store of value. We use it first as the *medium of exchange;* goods and services are paid for in money, and debts are incurred and paid off in money. Without money, economic transactions would have to take place on a barter basis. Thus money facilitates the exchange process. Second, the values of economic goods and services are measured in money. Money as a *measure of value* makes possible value comparisons of goods and services and the summations of quantities of goods and services on a value basis. Concerning this last point, it is not possible to add apples and oranges, but it is possible to add the *values* of apples and oranges. Third, wealth may be held in the form of money. Money balances held by people in demand deposits at banks or at home in a sock are noninterest-bearing assets. Money serves as a *store of value.*

Economists use the words *money supply* to mean the quantity or stock of money in the economy. The nation's money supply is composed of demand deposits (checking accounts) and currency in circulation (paper currency and coins). Table 10–2 shows the breakdown of the money supply between demand deposits and currency and the growth in the money supply since 1960.

TABLE 10–2
Movements in the money supply in selected years 1960–1978
($ billions, seasonally adjusted)

Year (December)	Total money supply	Currency	Demand deposits
1960	144.2	29.0	115.2
1962	150.9	30.6	120.3
1964	163.7	34.3	129.5
1966	175.8	38.3	137.5
1968	202.5	43.4	159.0
1970	219.7	49.1	170.7
1971	234.0	52.6	181.5
1972	255.3	56.8	198.4
1973	270.5	61.5	209.0
1974	282.9	67.8	215.1
1975	295.2	73.7	221.5
1976	313.5	80.7	232.8
1977	338.5	88.6	249.9
1978	361.1	97.5	263.6

Source: *Economic Report of the President, January, 1979*, p. 251.

The equation of exchange

A simple way of establishing the relationship between the money supply and the price level is provided in the following equation: $MV = PT$, in which M is the money supply, V is the velocity of circulation or the number of times the average dollar is spent per year, P is the price level or price index, and T is the physical volume of goods and services traded per year. The equation states that the supply of money times the velocity of money equals the price times the quantity of goods traded. Another way of looking at the equation is that the amount of money spent (left-hand side of the equation) equals the value of the goods sold (right-hand side of the equation). Surely no one doubts that the monetary value of purchases must equal the monetary value of sales. Then what is the importance of the equation of exchange?

Quantity theory of money

The equation of exchange is the starting point for the understanding and development of the *quantity theory of money*. This theory places prime importance on changes in the money supply. It states that the price level and output tend to move in the same direction as the money supply. Now return to the equation. If the money supply increases and the velocity of money stays the same, prices and output must rise. In these circumstances, if the economy were at full employment, an increase in the money supply would bring a proportionate rise in prices.

This is the same conclusion arrived at in the preceding chapter in the discussion of aggregate-demand analysis. An increase in aggregate demand, assuming full employment, will increase prices only. The quantity theory of money is an alternative way of explaining and understanding the economic forces determining prices, output, and employment in the economy.

The quantity theory of money stresses a couple of points that may have been overlooked in the previous analysis. Inflation due to a demand pull is possible only if the money supply expands, or the velocity of circulation increases, or both. It is usually correct to say that behind every great inflation there is a relatively great expansion in the money supply. In the next section on the causes of inflation, it is assumed that the money supply increases with increases in demand for money.

CAUSES OF INFLATION

Before policies can be designed to deal with inflation, the causes of inflation must be understood. We know from the quantity theory of money that a *basic* cause of inflation is *excess* aggregate demand generated by expansions in the money supply. Are there other causes?

Demand-pull inflation

Economists agree that most inflations are demand-pull inflations. This type of inflation is initiated by an increase in aggregate demand and is self-enforcing by further increases in aggregate demand. A demand-pull inflation is associated with increases in production and employment until the economy reaches full employment. Once full employment is reached, further increases in demand increases prices only.

Figure 10–1 depicts a demand-pull inflation. Beginning at the price level p and production q, an increase in aggregate demand to D_1 means that all of demand cannot be satisfied at p. Thus, the price level rises to p_1, and production rises to q_f. Then demand increases to D_2, causing the price level to rise further to p_2. This inflationary process continues as long as aggregate demand increases, since all of demand can be satisfied only at higher prices. Pure inflation, an increase in the price level without an increase in output, is shown when aggregate demand increases to D_2.

Cost-push inflation

It is difficult to explain some of the inflationary periods in the 1960s and 1970s only on the basis of a demand-pull inflation. The economy

FIGURE 10–1

Demand-pull inflation

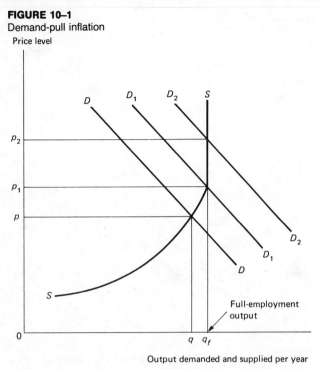

Demand-pull inflation is due to increases in aggregate demand from DD to D_1D_1 to D_2D_2.

experienced both inflation and recession together at certain times. How can this be? A demand-pull inflation is characterized by *rising* prices and *rising* production until full employment is reached. Inflation and recession at the same time mean *rising* prices and *falling* production.

The only way the economy can experience simultaneous inflation and recession is for inflation to be initiated by a decrease in aggregate supply. This type of inflation is called *cost-push inflation*. Increases in costs cause aggregate supply to decrease, which reduces the quantity of goods produced and increases prices.

Figure 10–2 illustrates a cost-push inflation. Beginning at price level p and production q_f, aggregate supply decreases to S_1. Now all of demand cannot be satisfied at p; that is, aggregate output demanded is greater than aggregate output supplied. As a consequence, the price level rises to p_1. Aggregate supply decreases further, to S_2. Again, all of demand cannot be satisfied, and price rises to p_2. This inflationary process continues until there are no further decreases in aggregate supply. It can be observed in Figure 10–2 that a cost-push inflation is characterized by rising prices and falling production.

FIGURE 10–2
Cost-push inflation

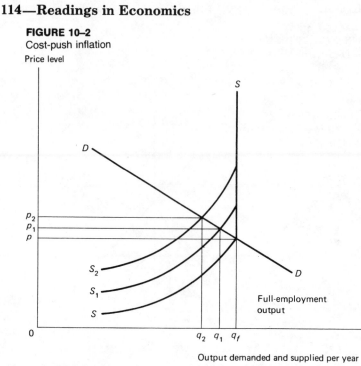

Output demanded and supplied per year

Cost-push inflation is due to a decrease in aggregate supply from SS to SS_1 to SS_2.

A demand-pull inflation is explained in terms of theory—aggregate-demand theory and the quantity theory of money. A cost-push inflation is explained in terms of the market power possessed by unions and producers in certain industries. In highly monopolized industries, unions and management may use their market power to determine wages and prices independently of market forces. One explanation is that unions increase wages in excess of productivity increases. The effect of this is to increase labor cost per unit of output. With control over price and production, producers respond by decreasing supply and shifting higher unit labor costs to consumers in the form of higher prices.

Demand-pull and then cost-push inflation

It may be misleading to look upon demand-pull and cost-push as two separate inflationary processes. They may be part of the same one, in that a single inflationary period may consist of both demand-pull and cost-push pressures.[4] Increases in aggregate demand start the inflationary process. Prices, production, and employment rise in response to the pull of demand. Money wages rise, but with a lag behind prices. Unions realize eventually that wages have lagged behind prices and begin to try to catch up by demanding wage increases in excess of productivity increases. Once this happens, cost-push pressures begin to reenforce demand pressures.

The end of an inflationary process may not coincide with the moment that demand-pull pressures no longer exist. Prices may continue to rise for a period because of cost-push pressures. These pressures operating alone sustain the inflation temporarily, even though production and employment are falling. However, without demand-pull pressures, inflation eventually stops.

CONTROL OF INFLATION

With reference to the equation of exchange—$MV = PT$—inflation results when MV is rising faster than T. Consequently, it should be controllable if one or more of these variables can be controlled. During an inflationary period M almost invariably is expanding, causing an increase in MV, or aggregate demand. The velocity of circulation, V, is also likely to be expanding, reflecting a decrease in people's desires to hold onto their money when it is going down in value. The volume of trade, T, reflecting primarily the total output of the economy, tends to increase if there are unemployed resources in the economy. However, its rate of increase will be impeded if the factors underlying cost-push inflation are present. In this section we shall consider how these variables can be controlled by means of monetary policy, fiscal policy, and the antimonopoly policy of the federal government.

Monetary policy

Monetary policy refers to the control exercised over the money supply, M, by the federal government. Demand deposits are far and away the largest component of the money supply—in 1978 the average amount of demand deposits in existence was $263.6 billion, while the average quantity of the currency was $97.5 billion. Therefore they represent the immediate target of control measures. How is control of the amount of demand deposits available for use accomplished? To

---

[4]Samuel A. Morley, *The Economics of Inflation* (Hinsdale, Ill.: Dryden Press, 1971), pp. 4–6.

answer this question, we must sketch out the structure and operation of the U.S. banking system.

Creation of demand deposits.   The hundreds of commercial banks in which we have our checking accounts and do our borrowing generate the demand deposit component of the money supply. Demand deposits come into existence in two ways. First, when we deposit currency in our banks, the demand deposits of the banking system are increased by the amount deposited. Second, when we borrow from our banks, they give us the loans in the form of additions to our checking accounts, thus generating new demand deposits.

Deposits arising when we take currency to the banks do not increase the total money supply, M. The currency turned over to the bank is no longer in circulation, so M is decreased by that amount. The deposits generated are equal in amount to the currency turned over to the bank. The whole process is a straightforward exchange of currency for demand deposits, with no net change in M.

Deposits arising from borrowing are a different story. When we borrow we give our banks promissory notes—which are not money. In exchange, the banks increase our demand deposits—our checking accounts—by the amount borrowed. These additions to demand deposits are money, so the lending activities of banks serve on balance to increase M.

The deposit component of the money supply is decreased by the inverse of the process discussed above. When we need currency we write checks to "cash." Our banks give us the currency and reduce our bank accounts by the same amount. Note that this does not change M, however. When we repay bank loans, we write checks to our banks—thus reducing our demand deposits. They give us nothing in return but our canceled promissory notes! So this process operates to reduce M.

Three fundamental principles characterizing the effects of commercial bank operations on M emerge from the foregoing discussion. First, when commercial banks are making new loans in greater amounts than old loans are being paid off, demand deposits and, consequently, M will be expanding. Second, when the amounts of new loans being made are less than the amounts of old loans being paid off, M will be contracting. Third, when the amounts of new loans being made are just equal to the amounts of old loans being paid off, M is neither expanding nor contracting.

Unfortunately, when banks are left to follow their own individual interests, their actions augment inflationary forces. It is precisely when economic expansion and inflation are occurring that it is most profitable for banks to expand their loans. Business firms want to borrow, and their demands for loans raise the interest rates that banks can charge. The dangers of defaults by borrowers are minimal. The resulting increases in M add fuel to inflationary fires.

Federal Reserve control of demand deposits. The federal government has sought to limit this economically perverse tendency of commercial banks by means of the Federal Reserve System established by the Federal Reserve Act of 1913. Under the act 12 Federal Reserve banks were established—one in each of the Federal Reserve Districts into which the United States is divided. These act in a coordinated way as the central bank of the United States, with their activities controlled by a seven-member Board of Governors. A central bank acts as a banker's bank. Commercial banks themselves hold deposits at Federal Reserve banks and may also borrow from them. A second function of a central bank is to control the demand deposits that exist in the economy.

The bulk of the total demand deposits of individuals and businesses at commercial banks is held in banks that are members of the Federal Reserve System. Many commercial banks are national banks, receiving their charters from the federal government. All these are required by law to be members of the system. The rest are state banks, chartered by individual states. Membership in the Federal Reserve System is optional for them, but it offers sufficient advantages so that many elect to join.

The feature of commercial banks that enables the Federal Reserve Board of Governors to exercise control over their total demand deposits is the reserves that they hold against their deposits. Reserves are in the form of commercial bank deposits at Federal Reserve banks, but they may also be held in the form of currency. The historical purposes of reserves are twofold. They serve to take care of both current routine needs of customers for currency and any extraordinary demands for currency that customers may have. The larger the ratio of a bank's reserves to the total demand deposits of its customers, the safer the bank is thought to be. Before the Federal Reserve Act was passed, experience indicated that prudent banking called for ratios of reserves to deposits—called *the reserve ratio*—of somewhere between 5 and 20 percent.

The Board of Governors can influence the quantities of reserves available to commercial banks and can set the minimum reserve ratio below which member banks of the Federal Reserve System cannot go. Both of these are indirect controls over the total volume of demand deposits in the economy.

To combat inflation, the Board of Governors can bring about reductions in the reserves of commercial banks through *open market operations* in government securities. Both commercial banks and Federal Reserve banks own large quantities of government bonds and treasury bills. By offering to sell at extraordinarily low prices, the Federal Reserve authorities can induce commercial banks to buy quantities of the securities from the Federal Reserve banks. Commercial banks use their reserves (deposits held at a Federal Reserve Bank) to buy them. As their reserves are reduced, so are their capacities to make new loans and to expand M.

A second means available to Federal Reserve authorities for reducing member bank reserves is elevation of the *discount rate*—the rate of interest charged commercial banks when they borrow from Federal Reserve banks. At any given time some part of total commercial bank reserves consists of such borrowing. When a member bank borrows from a Federal Reserve Bank it receives the loan in the form of a deposit at the Federal Reserve Bank; such deposits serve as reserves for member banks. Consequently, when Federal Reserve authorities raise the discount rate, making it more expensive for member banks to borrow, the total amount of member bank borrowing shrinks, making the total reserves of member banks smaller. This in turn reduces the capacities of member banks to make new loans and expands M.

A third method of reducing the tendency of commercial banks to expand demand deposits during periods of inflation is Federal Reserve control of the *minimum required reserve ratio* that member banks may hold. Suppose, for example, that the minimum required reserve ratio of member banks is 10 percent, total reserves are $50 billion, and total demand deposits are $250 billion. The actual reserve ratio of all banks together is 20 percent—$50 billion/$250 billion. If inflation is occurring, member banks could expand their total deposits to $500 billion, thus contributing to further inflation. However, if the Federal Reserve authorities increase the minimum required reserve ratio to 20 percent, the $50 billion in reserves will permit no expansion at all in new loans and demand deposits.

We should note that all three means available to Federal Reserve authorities for controlling demand deposit expansion during inflation can operate in reverse to encourage expansion of demand deposits during recession. Open market purchases of government securities by Federal Reserve banks will increase member bank reserves. So will decreases in the discount rate. Further, decreases in the minimum required reserve ratio will permit demand deposit expansion.

Fiscal policy

Fiscal policy refers to federal government decision making with respect to its tax receipts and its expenditures. The relative magnitudes of these factors have important effects on aggregate demand and, therefore, on the price level of employment in the economy. Given the level of government expenditures, increases in tax collections will reduce aggregate demand, whereas decreases in tax collections will increase it. On the other hand, given the level of tax collections, increases in government expenditures will increase aggregate demand, while decreases in government expenditures should provide means of attacking either inflation or unemployment.

When the economy is experiencing a period of inflation, the government can combat it by raising taxes, reducing expenditures, or both. To the extent that rising aggregate demand is causing demand-pull inflation, such measures will serve to slow or stop it. If, however, cost push is the primary cause of inflation, fiscal policies of this sort acting on aggregate demand will serve to increase unemployment at the same time that they slow down the rate of inflation.

Output expansion policies

Since inflation occurs whenever MV is increasing faster than T, it follows that anything that increases T or the output of the economy will be helpful in mitigating it. Obviously T can rise most easily when there is slack or unemployment in the economy, as there was in 1960. From 1960 through 1965 aggregate demand was increasing, but inflation was mild because T was increasing rapidly also. Once the economy approaches full employment of its resources, output expansions are difficult to achieve.

One possible way to encourage output expansion is through antimonopoly policies. Business monopolies tend to restrict production and hold prices higher than they would be in a more competitive economy. This can, of course, lead to unemployment of resources or an inefficient allocation of resources among different uses. Similarly, union labor monopolies tend to press wage rates higher, causing the employment level to be lower than it would be in their absence. Both business and labor monopolies tend to keep prices artificially high— higher than they would be under more competitive conditions.

A second way to encourage an expansion of the goods and services available to be purchased is through decreasing the restriction of imports from abroad. With reductions in tariffs and allowable quotas of foreign goods, more foreign goods will be imported and sold. These larger quantities amount to increases in T which help to hold the price level down.

THE INFLATION-UNEMPLOYMENT DILEMMA

A major problem in controlling inflation once it has gotten under way is that effective control measures almost inevitably cause unemployment. This happened as monetary and fiscal policies were tightened to control inflation from 1969 through the summer of 1971. By August 1971 what had been a 6 percent inflation rate was down to approximately 3.5 percent. But over the same period unemployment increased from less than 4 percent of the labor force to over 6 percent. This type of thing has led many people to raise the question: Can aggregate demand be controlled by monetary and fiscal policy so that the economy can operate at a stable price level and full employment?

The tradeoff problem

Some economists advance the argument that full employment and a stable price level are incompatible policy goals. They argue that an increase in aggregate demand, at less than full employment, will expand production and employment but will be associated with a cost-push inflation before full employment is reached. Also, they argue that an attempt to reduce inflation by reducing aggregate demand will prevent the economy from reaching full employment or move it away from full employment if it is already there.

Therefore, it is concluded that economic policies designed to control aggregate demand, such as monetary and fiscal policy, cannot achieve both full employment and a stable price level. Instead, there is a policy choice between full employment and some rate of inflation or between a stable price level and some rate of unemployment. This policy dilemma may be referred to as the tradeoff problem. How much unemployment should be traded for stable prices, or how much inflation should be traded for full employment?

Possible inflation-unemployment combinations

Paul Samuelson and Robert Solow studied the relationship between changes in the price level and changes in the unemployment rate in this country over a 25-year period and derived a tradeoff curve similar to the *TT* curve depicted in Figure 10–3.[5] The tradeoff curve shows the various combinations of inflation and unemployment that are possible, given the competitive behavior of buyers and sellers and the market structure of the economy. Look at points *A, B,* and *C* on the tradeoff curve *(TT)*. Point *A* shows a combination of a 3 percent unemployment rate and 5 percent inflation. Point *B* shows a combination of a 4 percent

[5]Paul A. Samuelson and Robert M. Solow, "Our Menu of Policy Choices," in Arthur M. Okum, ed., *The Battle against Unemployment* (New York: W. W. Norton & Co., 1965), pp. 71–76.

FIGURE 10–3
Possible combinations of inflation and unemployment

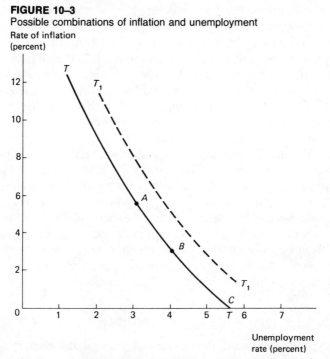

Any point on the tradeoff curve, *TT,* shows a combination of inflation and unemployment which is possible, given the degree of
competition in the economy. For example, point *B* represents a combination of 3 percent inflation and 4 percent unemployment, T_1T_1
shows an increase in the tradeoff curve.

unemployment rate and a 3 percent inflation, and point *C* a stable price
level associated with a 5.5 percent unemployment rate. Points between
A and *B* and *C* show other possible combinations of unemployment and
inflation.

The tradeoff curve indicates the policy choices. Can anything be
done to improve these choices, that is, to make stable prices and full
employment more compatible? In terms of the tradeoff curve, this
means a shift of the curve to be left, indicating a reduction in tradeoff
costs—a lower rate of inflation associated with any given rate of unemployment.

The evidence, however, is that the tradeoff curve has shifted to the
right since the Samuelson and Solow study. This means that higher
rates of inflation are associated with given rates of unemployment or
higher rates of unemployment are associated with given rates of inflation. In other words, the cost in the form of unemployment of main-

taining a stable price level has increased, or alternatively, the cost in the form of inflation of maintaining a 4 percent unemployment rate has increased. George Perry concluded from his study that at 4 percent unemployment the annual rate of inflation was 1.7 percent higher in the late 1960s than it was in the mid-1950s.[6] This increase in the tradeoff curve is shown in Figure 10-3. The 1974 recession casts some doubts that a tradeoff exists at all at times since in that year the economy experienced both rising prices and rising unemployment.

The tradeoff curve could be shifted to the left and even made to disappear if noninflationary monetary and fiscal policies were pursued and if the economy were perfectly competitive. Some inflation may be necessary to bring us out of a recession in which there is substantial unemployment. But over time, given monetary and fiscal policies that are not inflationary, people will come to expect and depend on stable prices. This in turn will induce them to price their goods and resources so that surpluses and unemployment do not occur. The more competitive the market structures of the economy, the more likely it is that stable prices and full employment will be compatible.

EXPERIENCES WITH WAGE-PRICE CONTROLS

The Nixon administration became convinced that monetary and fiscal policy could not cope with the economic situation existing in the economy in the summer of 1971. The economy was suffering from a high rate of inflation and unemployment. Although the rate of inflation was slowing down, it was argued that a new course of action was required to deal with both inflation and unemployment. The new course of action turned out to be a policy of wage and price controls.

The four phases

Phase One. A policy of wage and price controls was initiated by the Nixon Administration on August 15, 1971, with the announcement of a 90-day freeze period. The freeze period, Phase One, was followed by Phases Two, Three, and Four. During Phase One, plans were developed for the operation of a wage and price control scheme. Wages and prices did not rise much during the freeze period, since by government decree they were not supposed to increase. However, economic forces operating behind demand and supply are not affected by government decrees, and inflationary forces were continuing to build during the freeze period. In an attempt to explain why the freeze was a

---

[6]George L. Perry, "Changing Labor Markets and Inflation," *Brookings Papers on Economic Activity*, vol. 3 (1970), p. 433.

mistake, Milton Friedman stated, "Freezing individual prices and wages in order to halt inflation is like freezing the rudder of a boat and making it impossible to steer, in order to correct a tendency for the boat to drift one degree off course."[7]

Phase Two. Phase Two covered a 14-month period from November 14, 1971, to January 11, 1973. The wage and price control scheme was a mandatory scheme, that is, wage and price increases in industries under the controls had to be justified and approved by government. The wage and price guidelines were a 5.5 percent wage increase and a 2.5 to 3 percent price increase. The record during Phase Two was good if judged against these guidelines. During Phase Two food prices rose 6.5 percent, the cost of living increased 3.6 percent, and wages increased 5.9 percent.

Phase Three. Phase Three covered five months from January 11, 1973, to June 13, 1973. Under Phase Three the wage and price control scheme was voluntary. Wage and price guidelines were to be adhered to voluntarily, with the threat of government action in the event that they were not followed. Phase Three proved to be disastrous; wage and price controls completely broke down. This was partly because it was a voluntary scheme but primarily because of the adverse effects of price controls on supply and an increase in demand. The money supply rapidly increased during the period, making it possible for goods and services to be purchased at higher price levels.

Phase Four. A full cycle—from freeze to freeze—was completed on June 14, 1973, with the announcement of a 60-day freeze period. This was a half freeze, since some goods and services were not frozen (food and health) and some were frozen (meat, nonfood products, gasoline). After the 60-day freeze, on August 15, 1973, a system of mandatory wage and price controls was established. This marked the beginning of Phase Four. Phase Four, although a return to mandatory controls like Phase Two, may be remembered by its program of progressive decontrol. The purpose of the decontrol program was to provide for a smooth transition to a free market. By April 1974, when the last wage and price controls were dropped, many industries had already been exempted.

What have we learned from wage-price controls?

Our recent experiences with wage and price controls reflect some important lessons of economics. Lesson 1 is that a wage and price freeze does not prevent wage and price increases—it only postpones

---

[7]Milton Friedman, "Why the Freeze Is a Mistake," *Newsweek,* August 30, 1971, p. 22.

them. Lesson 2 is that a price control scheme that keeps market prices below market equilibrium prices creates shortages. Lesson 3 is that mandatory wage and price control schemes appear more effective than voluntary schemes, but both types of schemes treat the symptoms, not the cause, of inflation. Lesson 4, a concluding lesson, is that wage and price controls cannot resolve the inflation-unemployment dilemma.

RECESSION, RECOVERY, AND EXPANSION

The economy began slowing down in the last quarter of 1973—a slowdown that turned into a deep-seated slump in 1974 and 1975. The longest and costliest recession since World War II came to an end during the second part of 1975. Since then, the economy has bounced back and is expanding into 1979.

The recession of 1973–1975

The recession started with strong inflationary pressures operating in the economy and what was considered at the time a fairly high unemployment rate of 5 percent. Before the recession was over, the economy experienced an inflation rate of over 10 percent (1974) and an unemployment rate of 8.5 percent (1975). *Both* rising prices and rising unemployment that characterized the economy during the first year of the recession suggest that there were problems on the supply side of the market. Given aggregate demand, about the only way the rates of inflation and unemployment can move together is for there to be decreases in aggregate supply. Scarcities created during the time of wage-price controls and shortages of food and fuel in 1973 were basic causes of inflationary and recessionary forces existing side by side in 1974. This situation was not the inflation-unemployment dilemma that we have previously described. In 1974, there was no tradeoff between inflation and unemployment. We had high and rising rates of both.

Gardner Ackley, former chairman of the Council of Economic Advisors to the President, described the 1973–75 recession as a two-stage affair. The first stage, between the third quarter of 1973 and the second quarter of 1974, was characterized by declines in real consumer spending and residential construction. The basic cause of the decline in consumer spending was attributable to a decrease in the disposable income of consumers, primarily due to a $20 billion annual tax levied on them in the form of a unilateral rise in the price of imported oil.[8]

---

[8]Gardner Ackley, "Two-Stage Recession and Inflation, 1973–1975," *Economic Outlook USA*, vol. 2, no. 1 (Ann Arbor: University of Michigan Survey Research Center, 1975), p. 6.

During the second stage of the recession, between the second half of 1974 and the first quarter of 1975, declines in business investment occurred in response to further declines in real consumer spending and residential construction. With declines in business investment, in the form of spending both on plant and equipment and on inventories, a modest recession changed to a severe one.

The end of the recession was in evidence in the late spring of 1975 when certain leading economic indicators showed upward trends. Before the end came, recessionary forces slowed down the rate of inflation to about 5 percent. These same recessionary forces caused the highest unemployment since the Great Depression of the 1930s. At one time, the unemployment rate was approximately 9 percent (June 1975).

The 1975–1979 expansion

The economy bounced back from the 1974–75 recession and began expanding. The years 1976, 1977, and 1978 were characterized by increases in production and prices, and decreases in unemployment rates. Between 1975 and 1978, the average annual increases in the GNP in current dollars and in constant 1972 dollars were 12.6 percent and 6.1 percent, respectively, and the average annual rate of inflation based on the consumer price index was 7.1 percent. During the same period, the unemployment rate fell from 8.5 percent to 6 percent. Thus, the performance of the economy was not ideal since the rate of inflation was high, especially in comparison to past standards, and also the unemployment rate was not brought down to the full-employment benchmark rate of about 5 percent. Yet it can also be said that the economic record was not that bad either, since increases in the real GNP and employment expanded the living standards of many persons during this period.

The year 1979 is a critical year in the economy. Expansionary forces were dominating the economic scene when President Carter delivered to Congress the *Economic Report of the President* in January 1979. In his message to Congress, President Carter stressed an austere budget and made inflation the number one economic problem. Given inflation as the main problem, the aims of fiscal and monetary policy were clear, namely, to avoid the creation of excess demand and to slow down economic growth without producing a recession. Fiscal policy shifted to a policy of restraint in fiscal year 1979, the year beginning in October 1978, as the federal budget deficit was estimated to be reduced by about $11 billion when fiscal year 1979 is compared to fiscal year 1978. This restraining course of fiscal policy was projected to continue in fiscal year 1980, with the deficit expected to decline further.

Stagflation again?

In the beginning of 1979, there were mixed forecasts concerning how the economy would behave during the year. Some forecasts showed a recession before the year was over; some revealed a continuation of the expansion; and some models predicted a *growth recession,* that is, some growth but not enough to prevent unemployment rates from rising. The Michigan Model control forecast for 1979 was as follows: the real GNP would grow 2 percent, the rate of inflation would be 7.7 percent, and the unemployment rate would rise to 6.7 percent.[9]

These projected changes would add up to a growth recession for 1979. It seemed at the time that the forecast of the Michigan Model was realistic. However, economic events have taken place since the projection that could prove that even a growth recession is too optimistic for 1979. It appears now that the mid-year projection will show that the economy is heading toward a stagflation, that is, a recession accompanied by a high rate of inflation.

SUMMARY

Inflation means that the general level of prices is rising. It means that it takes more money to buy the same quantity of goods and services. Inflation may be suppressed. This occurs when quantity demanded is greater than quantity supplied at the current price level, but the price level does not rise because of government price controls.

The three effects of inflation are the equity, efficiency, and output effects. The equity effects involve the impact of inflation on income distribution. The people who lose during inflation are those receiving fixed incomes, holding assets in the form of money, and having fixed money claims. The people who gain during inflation are those whose money incomes rise faster than prices and who hold assets which rise in value more than the increases in the prices of goods and services.

The efficiency effects of inflation involve the impact of inflation on the allocation of resources. Inflation changes the allocating of resources, since inflation alters relative commodity prices. It is not certain that this change in resource allocation is a less efficient allocation. However, some economists argue that the allocation of resources is distorted by inflation and results in a less efficient allocation of resources.

The impact of inflation on the national production of goods and

---

[9]*Economic Outlook U.S.A.,* vol. 6, no. 1 (Ann Arbor: University of Michigan Survey Research Center, Winter 1978–79), p. 4.

services (output effects) may be to encourage production. Before the economy reaches full employment, rising prices tend to go hand in hand with rising production. The same forces that cause prices to rise cause production to rise. However, the continuation of inflationary forces at full employment leads to pure inflation, that is, rising prices not associated with rising production.

It is very important not to allow inflation to get out of hand. Whereas a steady rate of inflation of 5 percent per year may not be the ideal situation, it does not represent the kind of problem that an accelerated inflation does. The key to controlling inflation is to control the growth in the money supply. The growth in the money supply may be controlled by Federal Reserve monetary policies.

The economic situation in the summer of 1971, rising prices and high unemployment rates, brought on an era of wage and price controls. This era lasted until April 1974. Some important economic lessons learned from the 1971–74 experiment with wage and price controls are: (1) wage and price controls only postpone wage and price increases; (2) a price control scheme may create shortages; (3) a mandatory wage and price control scheme appears more effective than a voluntary scheme; and (4) wage and price controls cannot resolve the inflation-unemployment dilemma.

The economy experienced both an inflation and a recession in 1974 and 1975. Shortages in fuel and food and slumps in the housing and auto markets were contributing factors. The pace of the inflation slowed down by the summer of 1975, and the economy began to recover from its worst recession in over 30 years. Since the recovery in mid-1975, the economy has been expanding. Between 1975 and 1978, the average annual growth rate of the real GNP was 6.1 percent, the rate of inflation averaged 7.1 percent yearly, and the unemployment rate was reduced to 6 percent. The expansion will probably end in 1979, and on the horizon, it appears that a repeat of the 1974–75 stagflation is a likely happening.

READING 11

The Role of Supply-Side Economics in Fighting Inflation

During the past several years, a profound revolution has been occurring in the thinking of many of our nation's leaders concerning the proper role of fiscal policy in helping to maintain the health of our economy. For more than 30 years, our government tried to use fiscal policy as a means of smoothing out fluctuations in business activity. Tax rates were cut, and expenditures increased, when recessionary forces were pervasive. Growth in expenditures was restrained—and, on one occasion, tax rates were increased—to cool off inflation.

Deep disillusionment has set in regarding the results of those efforts. As the prestigious Joint Economic Committee (JEC) stated in its mid-year *Report* on the economy, a review of the postwar period shows that "government attempts to shorten the duration or reduce the intensity of recessions...have been ineffective." Economic policy for the future, the JEC argues, "must focus on the supply side of the economy, on the long-term capacity to produce...."

Supply-side economics is an exciting doctrine. Its central tenets are not entirely new, but they certainly are relevant. Our principal economic problem today is inflation. A long-term strategy is needed to deal with it.

Supply-side economics in fiscal policy is a logical complement to the way in which monetary policy is currently being conducted. In October 1979, the Federal Reserve announced that it was changing its methods of implementing monetary policy in ways that would improve its control over the expansion of money and credit. Under this new monetary policy strategy, prospects have been enhanced that growth of money and credit will slow over the long run to rates that are consistent with a moderation of inflation, and eventually a restoration of price stability. If fiscal and monetary policies both aim at reducing inflation over the long run, the prospects for success in this effort will surely be greater.

How much help can we really expect from supply-side economics in curing inflation? As I think about that question, I cannot help but remember the enthusiasm with which economists of my generation embraced the old fiscal doctrines 30 years ago. We spent a large part of our energy elaborating the theory of aggregate demand management, as it was so often called, and testing its conclusions against the facts. We tried our best to make fiscal policy work in ways that would reduce unemployment and idle capacity, keep the economy operating close to its full-employment potential, and yet avoid periods of excess demand that create fresh inflationary forces.

In retrospect, our principal mistake was a failure to recognize the severe limitations of aggregate demand management in an economy as complex as ours. We tried to achieve results that simply could not be realized.

The same danger exists now, I believe, with supply-side economics. Steps to increase the potential output of our economy and to improve productivity can make a vital contribution to dealing with inflation. However, unless we recognize the limits of supply-side economics, and design our economic policies accordingly, we could end up making our inflation problem worse instead of better.

What do we mean by supply-side economics? Conceivably, a wide range of things could be included—energy policy, manpower training, federal support for higher education, and other programs that might increase the growth of supply or enhance productivity. I propose to focus today on three principal areas in which public discussion of supply-side economics has centered in the past several years: first, tax reductions on earned income—that is, on wages and salaries—to increase incentives to work; second, tax incentives to businesses to increase the rate of capital formation and thereby to improve productivity; and third, tax reductions on investment income to encourage a larger volume of private savings.

In discussing these three ways to increase aggregate supply, I do not propose to break any new ground. My objective is merely to make some common sense observations on the potential contribution of this fiscal policy approach to solving our inflation problem.

Tax Reductions on Earned Income

Tax reductions for wage and salary income, if they contributed to the fight against inflation, would certainly have the enthusiastic support of a large number of our citizens. The average American gives up about one-fifth of his income in the form of direct tax payments to government; upper-bracket rates are, of course, much higher—up to 70 percent for the federal personal income tax. Reducing these tax rates significantly might increase the willingness of individuals to work, and it could do so in a variety of ways—by increasing hours worked per day or per week, inducing larger numbers of women to enter the labor force, encouraging postponements of retirement age, or making people willing to work harder. Is it possible that the aggregate supply of labor, and hence the output of goods and services, would rise substantially as a consequence of such tax reductions?

A bit of thought and introspection should raise some doubts in our minds. Work hours tend to be set by institutional arrangements as much as by individual decisions. Objectives for working, moreover, are complex and varied; many of us work for reasons other than simply the income we earn. Moreover, it is difficult to predict whether a completely rational economic man would work more or less if taxes were lowered. Lower rates of taxation increase the take-home pay that can be earned from an additional hour of work or a second job, but they also make it possible to attain any given standard of living with less work.

Studies of the effects of taxation on the available supply of labor both in the United States and in other countries are numerous, but their conclusions are ambiguous. Even in countries where tax rates are considerably higher than in the United States, such as the United Kingdom, it is not clear that labor supply would increase if taxes were lower. In a summary of the available evidence two years ago, the Congressional Budget Office concluded that labor supply probably would increase if taxes on earned income in our country were reduced. The effect, however, would be small; total hours worked might increase by perhaps 1 to 3 percent for each 10 percent rise in after-tax wages.

Reductions in taxes on wages and salaries stimulate demands as well as supply. Estimates of the increase in demand that would result from such tax reductions are also controversial. Nonetheless, the available evidence indicates that the increase in aggregate demand would be substantially larger than the increase in aggregate supply, possibly five or ten times as large, or maybe more.

Tax reductions on wage and salary incomes, therefore, are not the most promising way to cure inflation. Indeed, unless the effects on aggregate demand were neutralized by raising other taxes or cutting budgetary expenditures, such tax reductions—if undertaken on any substantial scale—could make our inflation problem worse.

This does not mean that our government should be insensitive to the burden of taxation that Americans are bearing. Certainly, our chances for healthy economic growth will be greatly enhanced if the share of our national resources devoted to federal uses is reduced and the rate of taxation is lowered. But it does suggest that the principal contribution that supply-side economics can make to fighting inflation lies elsewhere.

Investment Incentives and Productivity

Providing tax incentives for business investment is another form of supply-side economics, one that we know more about. On several previous occasions during the postwar period, incentives to business capital formation have been increased through accelerated depreciation, or an investment tax credit, or a reduction in corporate profits tax rates. We therefore have some basis on which to judge their efficacy in stimulating capital formation and productivity growth.

A number of proposals have been put forward recently to stimulate investment through tax incentives. For example, in the administration's recently announced fiscal program, allowable depreciation rates for new plant and equipment would be increased by 40 percent, and the investment tax credit would be liberalized somewhat. The cost of these incentives, in terms of loss of federal revenues, would initially be small but would reach $25 billion per year by fiscal 1985. Corporate tax payments in that fiscal year would be reduced by about 17 percent as a result of the new tax incentives.

It has been estimated that these investment incentives would increase the long-term growth rate of productivity in our economy by about 0.4 percent per year—not right away, but after several years. Judging by studies of the effects of investment incentives introduced in the past, this is a fairly generous estimate, but a reasonable one. To put this amount of improvement in perspective, we might note that productivity in the past five years has been rising on average at about 1 to 1.5 percent a year. With an improvement of 0.4 percent, the trend would be up to 1.5 to 2 percent. If improvements in productivity growth occurred for other reasons as well, we might hope to regain the 2.5 percent average annual rise that characterized the first two decades of the postwar period. To put it another way, an improvement of 0.4 percent in annual productivity growth would lead, over the course of a generation, to an increase of 10.5 percent in the potential output of our economy. Such an increase would make possible a welcome improvement in standards of living, in addition to its potential contribution to moderating inflation.

Tax Incentives to Increase Savings

Increased investment expenditures, however, must be financed by increased savings. Otherwise, they, too, may add to inflation rather than reduce it. Let me turn next, therefore, to the third area of supply-side economics that I mentioned earlier: are reductions in taxes on investment income an effective way to increase savings?

Unfortunately, in this area, too, we do not know as much as we need to know to justify bold action. Like reductions in taxes on earned income, tax reductions on investment income cut two ways. By raising the after-tax earning power of every dollar saved, they increase the benefit to the consumer of postponing purchases today in order to increase buying power tomorrow. But because of that, they reduce the amount that a consumer has to save to assure his ability to achieve a given living standard later on.

No one knows for sure which edge of the blade cuts more deeply. Some studies have concluded that if our tax structure were changed in ways that reduced the taxation of investment income and raised the level of taxes on other forms of income, there would be no effect at all on private saving. Others suggest beneficial effects on private saving. This state of affairs should not prevent us from experimenting cautiously with changes in the tax structure that might encourage more saving. In light of the uncertainties, however, it is hard to imagine that tax incentives to foster savings can play more than a minor role in our battle against inflation, at least in the relatively near future.

Fortunately, there is a surer way of increasing the amount of savings available to finance a higher rate of business investment. It is an old-fashioned method, and one that has not been used much in the past two decades. It is to reduce the deficit in the federal budget through restraint on federal spending as rapidly as economic conditions warrant, and eventually eliminate it altogether. Surpluses in the federal budget, used to retire debt, would return funds to financial markets that could finance the additional business investment needed to improve productivity growth. That is also the way to increase the prospects that improved productivity growth will actually result in lower inflation. Let me turn to that issue next.

Productivity and Inflation

Increasing productivity growth through tax incentives for business investment appears to me to be the most promising route for moderating inflation through supply-side economics. But will it work? And how well?

Unfortunately, there is no guarantee that improved productivity will automatically reduce inflation. Indeed, among the major industrial nations of the world, rates of inflation during recent years have not been closely correlated with rates of productivity increase. From 1974 to 1979, for example, manufacturing productivity rose faster in France than in any other major industrial country. Yet, the rate of inflation in France during that period was higher than that for the United States and Canada, and far above that for Japan and West Germany.

How much an improvement in productivity contributes to reducing inflation depends on the responses of businesses and workers. If businesses do not, or cannot, increase their profit margins, the slower rise in costs that higher productivity brings will show up in smaller increases in prices. If workers then accepted smaller wage increases because inflation was moderating, costs would rise still more slowly and the inflation rate would come down further. The inflation rate might ultimately decline by two to three times as much as the initial increase in productivity.

The potential reduction in inflation made possible by a higher rate of advance in productivity will be realized, however, only if conditions in labor and product markets promote the necessary response in wages and prices. Product markets must be sufficiently competitive so that businesses are motivated to pass reductions in their costs through to lower prices. Markets for labor must be sufficiently slack so that workers are encouraged to accept smaller wage rate increases as the rise in prices moderates. That is why prudent monetary and budgetary policies—policies that aim for slower growth of money and credit and for movements of the federal budget toward surplus—are a necessary adjunct to supply-side economics. Unless these two work hand-in-hand, the promise that supply-side economics holds for reducing inflation could easily be lost.

Let me try to pull the threads of my argument together. Tax incentives to stimulate business capital spending appear to be the surest way of increasing our aggregate capacity to produce. At a cost of about $25 billion annually by 1985, in terms of revenue loss to the Treasury, we might reasonably expect productivity growth to increase by about 0.4 percent per year. Under favorable economic conditions, the inflation rate might be brought down by about 1 percentage point, or perhaps a little more, through this means. These are, I believe, realistic estimates of the costs and benefits of going the route of supply-side economics.

If the cost is that high, you may ask, is it worth it? I would respond: What better alternatives are there? Certainly, it is preferable to use tax policy to increase productivity and our capacity to produce than to try to squeeze out inflation by relying solely on highly restrictive fiscal and monetary policies, with the inevitable losses of jobs and real output that would be entailed.

Supply-side economics is obviously no cure-all for inflation. But the problem of inflation is so intractable that no single measure to deal with it will suffice. Our only hope for making substantial progress against inflaton over the next several years lies in keeping the fight against inflation at the forefront of every economic policy decision. If we recognize its limitations as well as its strengths, supply-side economics can play an extremely useful role in that endeavor.

READING 12

The Economics of Bigness: Who Does What to Whom?

The great day arrived at last. For two years Dave Jones had suffered an unrequited love affair with the low-slung Model Z of the Ace Automobile Corporation. The sticker was the $8,500 price tag. College expenses were in competition for the money he had earned since graduating from high school. But now, just before returning to State University for his third year, it looked as though he had it all together. Acquiring a $4,000 loan from the local bank was the last link in the chain, and he had finally convinced the loan department that he could maintain payments on that amount. Dave hurried through breakfast and took the bus downtown to the local Ace Agency. Together with the salesperson he went over the specifications of the car that he wanted. When the bill of sale was drawn up and handed to Dave, he simply could not believe what he saw! The bottom line was $9,350! The salesperson explained patiently and carefully the recent 10 percent increase in Model Z prices.

How could one of the major manufacturers of automobiles get away with this kind of thing? Don't the big enterprises of the country have any regard for the thousands of people that keep them in business? Dave felt crushed and powerless. And he had a rising conviction that control over the economy rested with giant business firms, not with people like himself.

THE PUBLIC VIEW OF BIG BUSINESSES

The general public is highly suspicious of how big business enterprises behave. In fact, it is suspicious of bigness in general. Its disillusionment with big government, growing over the years since the Great Depression and World War II, was given a great boost by the Watergate scandals that cost Richard Nixon his job. It continues to be expressed by pressure on legislative bodies to hold down the taxes and expenditures of government units. But public concern with big business goes much further back—at least as far back as the era of the "Robber Barons" in the last half of the 1800s. What are the reasons for public animosity toward big businesses? There are several possible answers—all of them related.

First, many people believe that economic activity is dominated by a few gigantic firms. They think that families and individuals have little or nothing to say about their own economic destinies or about the paths that economic events take over time. They feel impotent and frustrated, sensing that it is big business that wields the economic power.

Second, there is a strong suspicion that big businesses deliberately hold back outputs. This feeling comes to the forefront whenever there are shortages. Housing shortages are attributed to "holding back" by construction firms and realtors. During the recent natural gas shortages, gas companies were accused of withholding supplies. The gasoline crunch of the summer of 1979 was believed by many to have been contrived by the major oil companies.

Third, it is commonly thought that big businesses can charge whatever prices they please for their products. Steel companies, automobile companies, oil companies, and even the makers of breakfast cereals are believed to have the power to set prices in blatant disregard of consumer interests. In fact, many believe that inflation is caused by the exercise of such power and that wage-price guidelines will help to contain it.

Fourth, big businesses are thought to earn exorbitant profits—"obscene profits" is the term sometimes used in the newspapers. These profits presumably are made at the expense of (1) consumers who are charged prices that are too high and (2) employees who are paid wages and salaries that are too low. The relationship of presumed excessive profits to the other three beliefs about bigness is obvious.

THE ECONOMICS OF MONOPOLY POWER

In a nutshell the public is concerned about the exercise of monopoly power by big businesses. To think in a systematic way about the problem and to understand what kind of threat, if any, big businesses pose we look first at what constitutes monopoly power. Then we analyze its impact on outputs and prices. Next, we examine the profit issue. Finally, we turn to the effects that monopoly power can have on the operation of the economy.

What is monopoly power?

As usually defined, *monopoly* in its strictest sense means there is a single seller of a good or service for which there are no good substitutes. Not many big businesses fit the full conditions of this definition, however. Most large enterprises operate in industries in which there are several other firms producing and selling its product. In general texts label such a market structure one of *imperfect competition*. It is the monopoly power exercised by firms in imperfectly competitive as well as monopolistic markets that people worry about and to which we should address ourselves in this chapter.

The monopoly power of a firm refers to the extent of its control over the supply of the product that is produced by the industry of which it is a part. The more firms there are producing and selling a given product, the less control any one of the firms can exercise over industry supply. If there are enough firms in an industry so that one firm's output and its control over industry supply are insignificant, we have a competitive market. On the other hand, if there is only one firm producing and selling the product, we have a market of pure monopoly. The monopoly power of a firm in an imperfectly competitive market is greater the larger the firm's output is relative to the output of the industry as a whole. It is less the smaller the firm's output is relative to the output of the entire industry.

Outputs and prices

What impact does monopoly power have on the price a firm charges and on the output level it produces and sells? A useful approach to the question is to contrast the price and output of a firm that exercises monopoly power with those of a firm that does not—that is, with a competitive firm.

Demand. We look first at demand for the product being sold. Figure 12–1 illustrates a typical market demand curve. It can be established immediately that with any market structure—competitive, monopolized, or imperfectly competitive—sellers must take into account what buyers will do. For quantity x_1 per unit of time, buyers will pay a price not higher than p_1. If sellers try to raise price above p_1, say to p_2, they cannot sell quantity x_1. At the higher price they can sell quantity x_2 only. Consequently, we conclude that the price that sellers are able to

FIGURE 12-1

A market demand curve

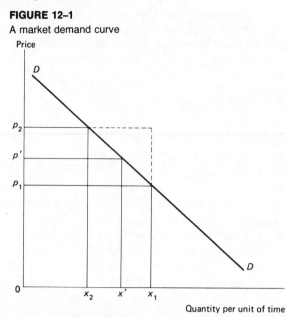

A firm in a monopolized market faces a downward sloping curve like DD for its output. Consumers will not pay more than p_1 per unit for an output of x_1 per unit of time. In order to raise the price to p_2 the monopolist must reduce the total sales level to x_1 per unit of time. If four firms of equal size were producing output level x_1 one of the four could cause the product price to rise to p' only by cutting its output and sales to zero.

charge is always limited by what buyers are willing to pay. Sellers cannot escape the law of demand.

The more sellers there are in the market for a product, the less control any one seller has over the price that it can charge. Suppose, for example, that in Figure 12-1 four sellers of approximately equal size are selling quantity x_1. By how much can any one of the four raise product price? If one firm reduces its output and sales to zero, the other three firms would be selling a total of approximately x' per unit of time and the price would be p'. Price p', then, is the highest level to which any one of the four firms acting independently can force the price and it can do this only if it ceases to produce. To stay in business it must of necessity charge less.

Using the same reasoning, if there were 100 sellers in the market, the power of one seller to raise the price would be much less. If there were 1,000 sellers, one seller would not be able to affect the market price of the product at all. If it were to drop out of the market, the total amount sold would decrease by only 1/1000 of x_1, which is not enough to cause the price to rise perceptibly. This latter case is typical of a competitive selling market.

Profit maximization. Economic entities such as consumers, resource owners, and business firms like to do the best they can with what they have. Consumers like to get as much satisfaction as possible from spending their annual incomes. As resource owners we like to get as much income as possible from selling or hiring out the labor and the capital we own. Similarly, business firms try to set prices and output levels so as to make as much profit as possible. As a matter of fact, the profit maximization principle is an integral part of the attempts of resource owners to get as much income as they can from their resources.

Profit maximization is not a goal peculiar to firms that have monopoly power. It tends to be a major objective of firms in all types of market structures. It is simply the logical conclusion that economic entities reach because they prefer more to less and make their choices accordingly. Although profit maximization is undoubtedly a major goal of business firms, it is not necessarily the only goal. Firms may also want to build up goodwill in a community, do right by their employees, or be known for a quality product. They may also want to get rid of their rivals, collude to raise prices, or block entry into the industry.

In any case prices and outputs tend to be set so as to maximize profits (or minimize losses) regardless of whether firms producing and selling the product are competitive or have monopoly power. But monopoly power, as we shall see, has important implications for what those prices and outputs will be.

Price and output in a competitive market. How does a firm in a competitive market determine what price to charge and what output to produce? Consider the market diagram in Figure 12–2. This is an ordinary market demand and supply diagram. The market price is p_x and the market output is X. But one individual firm selling this product has *no price-setting capabilities whatsoever* since it supplies an insignificant part of the total market supply. The individual competitive firm can determine only the quantity per unit of time to sell at the market price p_x.

The competitive firm faces the *horizontal demand curve dd* for its possible outputs. Its level is determined by the market price of the product. Suppose the market price is $14. In Table 12–1 column (4) represents the demand schedule facing the firm, and column (5) shows the firm's total revenue *(TR)* at output levels up to ten units per day. Although the numbers in column (6) are the same as those in column (4), the concept of marginal revenue for the firm differs from the concept of price. *Marginal revenue (MR)* is defined as the change in total revenue resulting from a one-unit change in the output level. The significance of this concept will become apparent shortly.

FIGURE 12–2

Price and output determination in a competitive market

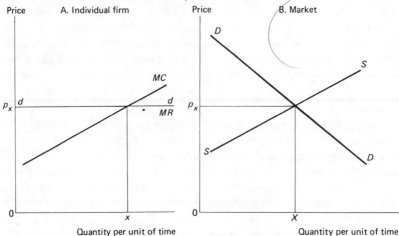

Product price p_x is determined in the market by the interaction of all buyers and all sellers. The individual firm faces the horizontal demand curve *dd*, which is also the firm's *MR* curve. The firm maximizes profits by producing output level *x*. Altogether the many firms in the market produce output *X* in the market diagram. The market quantity scale is highly compressed relative to the firm quantity scale. The price scale is the same in both diagrams.

On the cost side, let column (2) in Table 12–1 represent the firm's total costs *(TC)* at different daily output levels. *Marginal cost (MC),* a concept used in the text, is the change in the firm's total cost resulting from a one-unit change in the output level.

Determination of the output level that maximizes the firm's profits is easy once we know its *TC* and its *TR* at each possible output. *Profits* (Π) are the difference between *TR* and *TC* at any given output level and

TABLE 12–1

Outputs, revenues, costs, and profits for a competitive firm

(1)	(2)	(3)	(4)	(5)	(6)	(7)
	Total	Marginal		Total	Marginal	
Output	cost	cost	Price	revenue	revenue	Profits
(X per day)	(TC)	(MC)	(P_x)	(TR)	(MR)	(Π)
1	$ 8	$ 8	$14	$ 14	$14	$ 6
2	17	9	14	28	14	11
3	27	10	14	42	14	15
4	38	11	14	56	14	18
5	50	12	14	70	14	20
6	63	13	14	84	14	21
7	77	14	14	98	14	21
8	92	15	14	112	14	20
9	108	16	14	126	14	18
10	125	17	14	140	14	15

are listed in column (7). Profits are maximum at either six or seven units of output per day.

An alternative means of identifying the firm's profit-maximizing output is to find the output at which MR equals MR. Consider any output below the six-unit level, say three units. A one-unit increase in output would increase TR by \$14, or by the amount of MR. It would increase TC by \$11, or by the amount of MC. Therefore, it would increase Π by \$3, the difference between the MR and the MC of the fourth unit of output. Check the accuracy of this computation in the profit column. We have discovered an important principle: when MR is greater than MC, an increase in the output level will increase profits. Further increases in output through five and six units also increase profits since MR is greater than MC for each of the increases. An increase in output from six to seven units per day adds nothing to profits since $MR = MC = \$14$. However, it does not cause profits to decrease. If output is increased from seven to eight or more units per day, MR is less than MC and profits decrease—another important principle. But the most important principle of all is that profits are maximized by producing the output level at which MR equals MC. In Table 12–1 profits are maximum at an output level of seven units per day. To be sure, profits are also maximum at six units of product per day, but it will be easier to remember—and always correct—to settle on the output level at which MR equals MC.

The individual firm diagram of Figure 12–2 shows output x as the firm's profit-maximizing output. Note from Table 12–1 that if a firm's MR is plotted for each output, it will be a horizontal line coinciding with the firm's demand curve dd. The firm's MC curve can be thought of as column (3) of Table 12–1 plotted against output. The output level at which profits are maximum is the one at which MR equals MC.

The MC curve of the firm is the *firm's supply curve* for X, showing how much the firm will place on the market at alternative possible prices, other things being equal. In Figure 12–3 ignore for the present the market diagram and consider the individual firm diagram only. At a price of \$14, seven units per day will be produced and sold by the firm. What would the firm do if the price were \$10 instead of \$14. The firm's demand curve and MR curve become d_1d_1 and MR_1, respectively. The profit-maximizing output level falls to three units per day. Since the firm seeks to maximize its profits, whatever the market price happens to be, the firm will try to produce the output at which MC equals MR. For a competitive firm MR and p_x are always equal, so in producing the output level at which MC equals MR, the firm is also producing the output level at which MC equals p_x. Thus, the outputs that will be produced at alternative price levels are shown by the MC curve, making it the firm's supply curve for the product.

By adding the quantities that all firms in the market will place on the market at each possible price, we get the *market supply curve*. For example, in Figure 12–3 if one of 1,000 identical firms in the market will place seven units of product per day on the market at a price of $14, all firms together will place 7,000 units per day on the market. In Figure 12–3 at the $14 price the firm would be at point *a* on its supply curve. The market as a whole would be at point *A*. Similarly at a $10 price level the firm would be at point *b* and the market as a whole would be at point *B*. The market *SS* curve is said to be the *horizontal summation* of the individual firm *MC* or *ss* curves. It is really a market marginal cost curve for all firms together.

The simultaneous determination of the market price of a product, the individual firm level of output, and the market level of output for a competitive market now falls neatly into place. In Figure 12–3 let the market demand curve be *DD* and the market supply curve be *SS*. The price of $14 is determined by the interaction of buyers and sellers in the market as a whole. It is this price that any one firm in the market takes as given and cannot change. To maximize profits the firm chooses the output level at which *MC* equals MR—seven units in this case. The market output level of 7,000 units is, of course, the sum of the output levels of all firms producing the product when they are confronted with a $14 product price.

FIGURE 12–3
Marginal costs and supply in a competitive industry

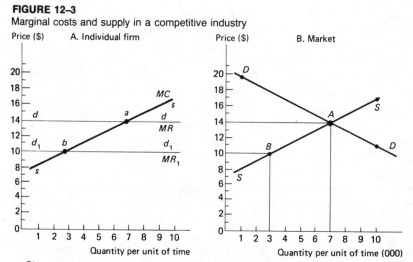

Since an individual firm produces the output at which $MC = MR = p_x$ in order to maximize profits, the firm's *MC* curve shows how much it will place on the market at alternative price levels like $10 and $14. The market supply curve shows the combined quantities that all firms in the market will supply at each alternative price. It is the horizontal summation of the *MC* curves of all the individual firms and is thus a market *MC* curve for the industry as a whole.

Pricing and output in a monopolized market. To show the effects of monopoly power on the price and the quantity produced of a product, we will suppose that the purely competitive market just discussed becomes monopolized. The market demand curve *DD* of Figure 12–3 is listed as a demand schedule in columns (1) and (4) of Table 12–2. Similarly the horizontal summation of the *MC* curves of the 1,000 individual competitive firms, which comprises the supply curve *SS* in Figure 12–3, is listed in columns (1) and (3) of Table 12–2. This information is presented again as *DD* and *(S)(S)* in Figure 12–4. As we noted in the preceding section, the market price of producing *X* is $14 and the quantity produced and sold is 7,000 units per day.

Now let the 1,000 competitive firms be merged into one gigantic monopoly. Suppose that all the production facilities of the 1,000 firms are taken over in their entireties and that they can be operated by the monopolistic firm with no loss in efficiency. What happens to the output of the industry and the price of the product?

Keep in mind how much the competitive firms were producing as they maximized their profits. Each firm found itself looking at a $14 product price that it could not change. Each firm saw a horizontal demand curve for its own output at the $14 level. Each firm viewed marginal revenue as constant at the $14 level—equal to the product price. Each firm produced an output level at which its *MC* was equal to *MR and product price*. Each firm's output level was seven units per day and the total industry output was 7,000 units per day.

All of that is changed by monopolization of the industry. The monopolist faces the market demand curve *DD*, which is downward sloping to the right instead of horizontal. This fact has important implications for marginal revenue. Any firm that faces a demand curve that is sloping downward to the right will find that its *marginal revenue is*

TABLE 12–2
Outputs, revenues, costs, and profits for a monopolized firm

(1) Output (000) (X per day)	(2) Total cost ($000) (TC)	(3) Marginal cost (MC)	(4) Price (P_x)	(5) Total revenue ($000) (TR)	(6) Marginal revenue (MR)	(7) Profits ($000) ($\pi$)
1	$ 8	$ 8	$20	$ 20	$20	$12
2	17	9	19	38	18	21
3	27	10	18	54	16	27
4	38	11	17	68	14	30
5	50	12	16	80	12	30
6	63	13	15	90	10	27
7	77	14	14	98	8	21
8	92	15	13	104	6	12
9	108	16	12	108	4	0
10	125	17	11	110	2	15

FIGURE 12-4

Comparison of pricing and output in competitive and monopolized markets

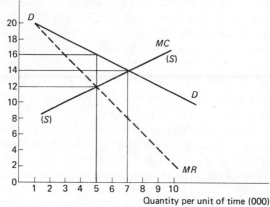

Price ($)

Quantity per unit of time (000)

If the market is competitive, the market price will be $14 and the output will be 7,000 units. Each of the 1,000 firms in the market faces a horizontal demand curve and marginal revenue curve at the $14 level and maximizes profits by producing the output at which its *MR* equals *MC*. Monopolization of the market causes the firm to see *DD* as the demand curve it faces. Since *DD* slopes downward to the right, *MR* lies below *DD*. The profit-maximizing output for the monopolistic firm becomes 5,000 units, which will be sold at a price of $16 per unit.

less than product price at any given output level. We demonstrated this principle in Table 12-2. If the monopolist were selling 2,000 units of product per day and were to increase sales from 2,000 to 3,000 per day, total revenue of the firm would increase from $38,000 ($19 × 2,000) to $54,000 ($18 × 3,000). Since the 1,000-unit addition to output increases total receipts by $16,000, each one-unit increase in output has increased *TR* by $16. So marginal revenue for the firm in moving from the 2,000-unit to the 3,000-unit level of output is $16 and is less than the price of $18 at which each of the 3,000 units is sold. Marginal revenue in column (6) is computed in the same way for each output level listed in column (1). Compare price and marginal revenue at each level of output. Marginal revenue is plotted as the *MR* curve in Figure 12-4.

If you were the monopolist, what output would you produce and at what price would you sell if your objective were to maximize profits? You would reduce output and sales from 7,000 units per day to 5,000 units per day. You would raise the price from $14 to $16. You would do this because it would increase your profits from $21,000 per day to

$30,000 per day as column (7) indicates. At the 5,000-unit output level, *MC* equals *MR* for the monopolist.

To recapitulate the analysis, in a monopolized market the price of the product tends to be higher and output tends to be less than it would be if the industry could be and were competitive. This is not because monopolized firms are inherently evil while competitive firms are not. The managements of firms in both types of markets seek the same general goal—profits. The monopolistic firm restricts output and charges a higher price because its managers see a different relationship between marginal revenue and price than do the managers of competitive firms.

Referring back to Figures 12–3 and 12–4, the managers of competitive firms face a demand curve horizontal at the market price of the product. Consequently they see a marginal revenue curve that is also horizontal and that coincides with the demand curve. To maximize its profits the competitive firm chooses the output level at which $MC = MR = P_x$. In the diagrams this occurs at the seven-unit output level for each firm. Since all firms in the market maximize profits in the same way, the market output is 7,000 units of output.

If the market is monopolized and the monopolist continues with the 7,000-unit output level, the monopolist's *MC* would be equal to the product price of $14. But *MR* for the monopolist at that output level is only $8 because the monopolist faces a downward-sloping demand curve. To maximize profits the monopolist cuts the output back to 5,000 units per day and raises the product price to $15. The monopolist's $MC = MR = $12 at that output level.

Entry restrictions

Prices, costs, profits, and losses in a private enterprise economy provide the incentives for a continuous reallocation of resources from uses where they contribute less to uses where they contribute more to consumer satisfaction. In industries where demand is falling or costs are rising, investors will eventually receive less than average returns on their investments. Firms in these industries are said to be incurring economic *losses*. As it becomes possible for them to do so, investors and the firms producing those products will leave the industry, reducing supplies and raising prices relative to costs, until the returns to remaining investors are average for the economy as a whole.

In areas where demand is increasing or costs are falling, investors receive higher than average returns, or economic *profits*. New investment and new firms have incentives to enter the industry. If they are successful in doing so, product supplies increase and prices fall relative to costs until the return on investment is again average. The profit and loss mechanism is thus the prime force for contracting productive capacity and output where these are not so urgently desired and for expanding them where they are more urgently desired.

Monopoly power tends to throw sand in the gears of the reallocation mechanism. Over time firms with monopoly power in profitable industries, those that yield higher than average rates of return to investors, may be able to impede or block the entry of new investment and new firms into those industries. To the extent that they are able to do so, outputs will be lower, prices will be higher, and profits will be greater than they would be if entry were open, free, and easy. Such barriers to entry can be classified conveniently into (1) private barriers and (2) government barriers.

Private barriers.   Private entry barriers arise from the nature of markets themselves or from marketplace actions of the firms that enjoy their fruits. There are many privately imposed restrictions on entry into specific industries. We shall list some of the more important ones—not necessarily in the order of their importance. First, consider a situation in which a firm or the firms already in a market own or control most of some key raw material needed for making the product. All they must do to restrict entry is to deny potential entrants access to it. Second, suppose that when new firms are in the process of entering, the existing firms threaten to lower prices to the extent that the newcomers would experience substantial losses. This threat tends to discourage entry. It is also tough on those already in the market, but they may be able to withstand temporary losses better than the potential entrants can. Third, product differentiation may be successful in retarding entry in some instances. *Product differentiation* refers to the well-known practice on the part of each firm in an industry of making its own brand of the product slightly different from that of the other firms. Then it tries to convince consumers that its brand of the product is superior to any other brand. Consumers tend to prefer the old tried and true brands and to be skeptical of purchasing the brands of new entrants. This is undoubtedly one of many factors discouraging entry into the automobile industry. Fourth, a market may not be large enough to support more than one or a few firms of a size large enough to be efficient. Though one or a few firms may be able to make higher-than-average returns for investors, the entry of a newcomer may increase supply and reduce prices so much that none makes an average return. The list of private entry barriers could go on and on, but the ones we have included should be sufficient for illustrative purposes.

Government barriers.   The firms already in specific industries have difficulty in policing and enforcing restrictions on entry. Consequently they frequently turn to the government for help. They get city councils, state legislatures, and Congress to pass legislation restricting entry into their markets. And those government units seem not at all reluctant to take actions that confer monopoly power on certain special interest groups and help them to maintain it over time.

First, in some industries such as railroads, trucking, airlines, and communications, regulatory commissions have established entry-blocking rules that have all the force of law. Initially regulatory commissions such as the Interstate Commerce Commission, the Civil Aeronautics Board and the Federal Communications Commission were established to "protect" customers from certain practices of monopolistic firms. Over time, however, the range of commissions' activities has expanded to include control of entry into the industries they are regulating. In recent years one could well suspect that their primary function is to "protect" the firms from consumers.

Second, there are many occupational licensing laws on the books of individual states licensing plumbers, undertakers, physicians, barbers, and many more occupations. Whatever else such laws may do, one thing is certain—they restrict entry into the licensed occupations. Licensing standards and licensing examinations usually are controlled by licensed members of the occupation concerned; that is, by those who are already in it and who have a vested interest in keeping the number of new entrants relatively low.

Many other forms of government-imposed entry barriers exist. Import duties and import restrictions limit the entry of foreign firms into many of our markets. Patent and copyright laws impede entry. Exclusive franchises to taxicab companies and casinos block the entry of new firms. Zoning ordinances and building codes are used to restrict entry into certain housing markets. Like the case of private barriers, the list of government-imposed barriers to entry is a lengthy one.

Nonprice competition

In industries containing only a few firms, it is common practice for firms to compete on grounds other than price. Each such firm in a given industry can increase its profits if it can increase its monopoly power at the expense of its rivals; that is, if it can increase its own share of the total market for the product. One very obvious way for a firm to increase its market share is to reduce the price at which it sells its brand of the product relative to the prices charged by the other firms in the industry. But price cutting presents dangers to the firm that does it. The other firms can cut their prices, too, thus preventing the first firm from accomplishing what it set out to do. Worse yet, all firms could end up with lower prices, a larger industry output, and smaller profits. So firms in imperfectly competitive markets are reluctant to use price cutting to increase their individual market shares. Usually they attempt to increase their degrees of monopoly power through nonprice competition.

Advertising is a major form of nonprice competition. Although it may provide consumers with important information about a firm's product, its major objective is to increase the market share or the monopoly power of the firm that does it. Unlike a price cut by the firm, a successful advertising campaign is hard for other firms to duplicate. Other firms will try to duplicate or match the advertising campaign of the first firm, but it takes time for them to do so. Meanwhile, the first firm reaps the rewards of its efforts. Eventually, if other firms succeed with effective campaigns of their own, all may end up with approximately the same market shares that they had before. Much of the advertising effort will have been wasted and, since the resources used for advertising purposes are not available to produce other goods and services, consumers receive a smaller total output from the economy as a whole.

Periodic change in the design and quality of the product is another major form of nonprice competition. Annual model changes fall in this category of activity. Model changes may incorporate new technological developments, and to the extent that they do so they enable given quantities of resources to make greater contributions to consumer satisfaction. But they may also simply rearrange or change the chrome and the shape, making old models obsolete and new models no better. Successful design and quality innovations by one firm, like successful advertising, may be hard for other firms to imitate immediately and may increase the market share and monopoly power of the firm for a time. However, if other firms are successful over time with their own design and quality changes, all may again end up with approximately the same market shares or with some rearrangement of market shares.

SHOULD WE FEAR BIGNESS?

Does bigness of business enterprises put our economic future in jeopardy? The economic analysis that we have just completed leads to the conclusion that in industries in which monopoly power is exercised, outputs will be lower and prices will be higher than they would be if the industries were more competitive. Monopoly power also may impede the entry of additional investment and firms into industries in which profits are made. Thus monopoly power may cause the resources or productive capabilities of the economy to be allocated poorly among alternative uses, with too little of the economy's resources allocated to the production of products made by industries in which monopoly power exists and with too much allocated to products that are produced competitively. In addition, monopoly power in imperfectly competitive markets may result in some waste of resources on nonprice competition.

Bigness and monopoly power

A business enterprise that is big in terms of the value of its assets or the value of its sales does not necessarily have a high degree of monopoly power. On the other hand, a relatively small firm may have a great deal of monopoly power. It all depends on the position of the firm in the market in which it operates. Chrysler Corporation is a very large firm in terms of its assets and annual sales volume; yet it appears to have very little monopoly power. If it drops out of the market, other firms will easily take up the slack. If it raises its prices relative to those of other firms in the auto industry, it will very quickly price itself out of the market. It has much actual and potential competition. Stillwater Power and Light Company in Stillwater, Oklahoma, is a small firm in terms of assets and annual volume of sales, but it comes very close to being a pure monopolist. It has no direct rivals, with the possible exception of the local gas company. We must therefore be careful not to confuse bigness with monopoly power.

Data are frequently cited to show concentration in U.S. business. For example, the largest 200 manufacturing firms in the United States owned 58.4 percent of the total assets of manufacturing firms in 1977.[1] This percentage is slightly greater than it was in 1960 and slightly less than it was in 1970. We learn very little from aggregate data of this sort. In assessing monopoly power of firms, we must look at specific industries and at individual firms within each industry to see whether or not they are able to affect significantly market outputs, prices, and buyers' access to the kind of product produced and sold by the industry. Correct interpretation of what is observed even then is very difficult in most instances.

Outputs and prices

We cannot be very certain in most imperfectly competitive industries whether or not firms are restricting outputs and holding prices up. For example, is there evidence in the automobile industry of output restriction? Hardly. Automobile prices have no more than kept pace

---

[1] U.S. Department of Commerce, Bureau of the Census, *Statistical Abstract, 1978,* p. 576.

with the rising average price level that we have been experiencing since 1965. Many accusations have been leveled at the refining stage of the petroleum industry. Every shortage of gasoline and fuel oil since 1973 has raised questions about whether it was "contrived" in order to raise prices. But the evidence seems to indicate that the shortages have resulted basically from price controls and from government allocations rather than from monopolistic conspiracy on the parts of domestic refining companies.

Although a monopoly firm in maximizing profits restricts output below the level at which MC equals p_x to a level at which MC equals MR, the very bigness that makes some monopoly power possible may also tend to offset its adverse effects either in part or in whole. Large firm size in many industries is necessary for efficient operation or for the use of mass production to achieve low per unit cost operations. In some industries a few large efficient firms may well give us more output at lower prices than would many smaller firms. Consider, for example, costs and prices that would be likely to result if the automobile industry were made up entirely of firms the size of American Motors with no Ford or General Motors companies in existence.

Entry restrictions and resource allocation

Economy-wide evidences of long-run misallocation of the economy's resources because of *private* entry barriers are rather difficult to find. In recent years we have seen many evidences of easy entry. Portable electronic calculators are a case in point. Simple early models commanded relatively high prices and were produced by two firms. But the success of the new product and the profits that were generated soon attracted new producers into the field. Supplies increased, prices fell, and the quality and sophistication of the units increased. The same sort of thing happened with digital quartz watches. By and large, private entry barriers to markets break down rather easily.

Where entry to markets is blocked by law it is easier to find evidences of resource misallocation. One of the more glaring instances of resources being used in quantities that are relatively too small is the medical profession. Physicians' average net incomes are at the top of the list for professions or occupations. Shortages of medical doctors have been publicly proclaimed for years and years. Yet, with their tight legal control of entry into medical training programs and into the profession itself, medical doctors continue to deter as many as half of the annual qualified applicants to medical schools from entering training. In many local building markets, housing costs have soared and profits to builders have been high because building codes have inhibited the introduction and use of new technology and prefabrication. In still another industry, try getting a taxicab in any large city during the morning and evening rush hours.

Nonprice competition

The impact of nonprice competition on the public is far from clear. The total expenditure on advertising for 1978 runs about $44 billion[2]—somewhere in the neighborhood of 2 percent of GNP. However, about one fourth of the total was for advertising in local newspapers, a type of advertising that provides information to consumers on what is available, where, and at what price. Another $9 billion was spent for television advertising and is not a total loss to consumers. It is payment—overpayment—for the "free" television programs that we see.

We also cannot be sure whether or how much the public loses from product design and quality changes. Many useful innovations are introduced in this way—the self-starter on the automobile (Yes, Virginia, they used to be cranked by hand), no-frost freezers and refrigerators, electric typewriters, and thousands of other items that make our lives more comfortable. But there are many others whose only purpose is to make the previous years' models obsolete.

Income distribution

How do bigness and monopoly power in the sale of products affect the distribution of income among economic units in the economy? It appears initially that, since entry into imperfectly competitive industries is restricted and since greater than average returns on investment may be obtained over time by firms in those industries, income is redistributed away from consumers toward those firms. Or, as it is commonly put today, those firms make monopoly profits. But on further investigation this possibility becomes shrouded in doubt. Big business firms are corporations, each having thousands of stockholders who are actually the owners of the business. The business enterprise itself provides a legal framework that enables these thousands of stockholders or investors to get together for purposes of production. Profits mean nothing to the enterprise itself. To the extent that the enterprise yields above average rates of return, those returns accrue primarily to its stockholders; they are really diffused among the thousands of households that own corporation stocks. Some of these—we do not know what proportion—are retired people, widows, old persons in rest homes, and the like; although, to be sure, the largest

---

[2]Robert J. Coen, "Ad Spending Is Outmuscling the National Economy in General," *Advertising Age*, January 8, 1979, pp. S-7 and S-8.

part of corporation returns to investors go to those in upper and middle income groups.

In addition, when a corporation yields higher than average returns on investment to its stockholders, its stock becomes attractive for people to buy. Increased demand for its stock drives stock prices up and the rate of return consequently becomes smaller and smaller to subsequent buyers of the stock. Only those stockholders who owned the stock at the time when the higher than average returns were made stand to gain.

We cannot really be sure that bigness of business enterprises results in a distribution of income that is more unequal than would be the case if all business firms were small.

SUMMARY

The general public tends to believe that big businesses exploit them. Many people think the economy is controlled by a few business firms and that these firms restrict product outputs and charge higher prices than they should. They also think that big firms make unjustifiable monopoly profits.

To the extent that an individual firm produces a significant part of an industry's output it can exercise some degree of monopoly power. Monopoly power induces firms to produce smaller outputs and charge higher prices than would be the case if the markets in which they operate were competitive. Firms with monopoly power are frequently able to restrict entry into their industries, thus compounding the output restriction and higher price problem and inhibiting valuations of resources from less valuable to more valuable uses. They also engage in nonprice competition which may result in the waste of some of the economy's scarce resources.

There is little evidence that bigness of business enterprises in the United States causes severe problems in the performance of the economy. Bigness does not necessarily mean monopoly power, and there is some question as to whether or not big businesses in general exercise monopoly power in significant degrees. In many fields big enterprises are simply more efficient than smaller ones. Some of the more serious abuses of monopoly power occur where the powers of government are enlisted to block entry into certain industries or occupations. Nevertheless, it is important that a close watch be maintained on potential monopolists. The more competition the economy can sustain, the better the price mechanism will operate in allocating the economy's resources among their many uses. But in many industries the exercise of some monopoly power is likely to be unavoidable for reasons of efficiency.

READING 13

Striking the Proper Balance in Regulation

That the pace and scope of the government's regulatory activity have increased sharply over the last decade is obvious. Whether and how the government should regulate certain activities have become familiar questions in policy debates. In the case of traditional economic regulatory activities, especially with regard to transportation, communications, and finance, there has been a growing recognition that we need to reduce direct regulation and give greater play to competitive forces. In these sectors regulatory reform has become synonymous with deregulation. But for the newer forms of regulation dealing with social concerns such as the environment, occupational health and safety, and the safety of consumer products, regulatory reform has come to mean not deregulation but more flexible and more cost-effective regulation. The government is increasingly seen to have a legitimate role in helping the private sector to attain socially desirable ends that cannot be achieved in the market place. People have also become much more aware that regulation often adversely affects productivity, at least as it is conventionally measured.

Over the last 3 years the Administration has made marked progress in reforming this country's regulatory institutions and procedures. In some cases regulatory structures existing for decades are being dismantled, exposing the industries they protected to new forces of competition. In other areas important procedural reforms have been put into place to help assure that, subject to legislative mandates, regulations set reasonable goals and meet those goals in a cost-effective manner. The job of reforming the regulatory process is far from complete, but an important beginning has been made.

REGULATORY POLICY AND PRODUCTIVITY

Government regulation of individual and corporate behavior takes many forms, including common law rules of liability, antitrust laws, restrictions on international trade, and regulatory rules of all kinds at the Federal, State, and local level. The ways in which this activity affects productivity are varied and complex, but several broad generalizations can be made:

First, regulations which divert capital and labor from the production of steel, automobiles, or clothing (where output can be readily measured) to the production of environmental cleanliness, workers' safety, or other goods whose values are difficult to measure, entail a loss in measured productivity. This is not necessarily a matter for concern, since it stems primarily from the limitations of what can be captured in the national income statistics.

Second, regulatory procedures which cost more in capital and labor than they yield in social benefits, or which require more resources than are necessary to meet stipulated social targets, do reduce national productivity, both measured and unmeasured.

Third, many economic regulations directly cut productivity. Before recent decontrol actions, airline regulations encouraged low load factors on airplanes. Current trucking regulations require needless empty backhauls and circuitous routing of trucks, both of which reduce productivity. Many local building codes necessitate the use of excessively costly materials. Perhaps an even more important cause of lower productivity is the attempt by many of the older economic regulatory bodies to preserve the domain of some established industries. Such protective measures can suppress the competitive pressures that force otherwise staid firms to adopt innovative ideas and improve their productivity.

Some loss in measured productivity is a necessary and unavoidable consequence of regulation. But there are also avoidable losses stemming from regulatory activities. Regulatory reform that works toward the elimination of outmoded economic regulations and promotes improvements in the balance and cost effectiveness of social regulation can contribute to growth in productivity.

REMOVING OBSOLETE REGULATORY STRUCTURES

The reasons why industries were originally made subject to detailed economic regulation regarding the prices they charged and the conditions under which they provided service were many and varied. One obvious example was the objection to the so-called "natural monopoly" enjoyed by an industry with such large economies of scale that meaningful competition was impossible. In other instances fear of "destructive competition" provided the primary rationale for regulation. Extending the scope of service was yet another aim behind government intervention. In many cases the original justification is no longer valid; in others it never existed. Legislative and administrative action is helping to remove these obsolete regulatory structures.

In late 1978, with the cooperation of the Congress, the Administration succeeded in opening up the domestic airline industry to meaningful entry and truly competitive pricing for the first time in at least 40 years. This was the culmination of a process of liberalization that had begun several years earlier. Under regulation, airlines competed through quality of service; under deregulation consumers benefited immediately from an expanded volume of flights and lower fares. By September 1978 the average level of domestic and foreign air fares for the 11 largest U.S. airlines had fallen 2.8 percent from the year before and stood only 1.4 percent above their 1976 level. In October 1978 air fares were actually lower than 2 years earlier.

Some critics have interpreted recent increases in airline fares as evidence that deregulation, though perhaps successful initially, will be a failure in the long run. Nothing could be further from the truth. Deregulation of an industry does not render it immune to increases in prices of factors of production. It does affect the degree to which such increases are translated into higher unit costs and prices. The airline industry has recently provided graphic proof of how reduced regulation can improve productivity and hence price performance.

As of the end of September 1979, average fares for the 11 domestic trunklines were 7.8 percent above their mid-1977 levels. But average weighted input prices for the airlines rose by 35.4 percent over this same period. These rises in input prices were largely offset by improved productivity. Load factors—the percentage of seats filled—rose from 56.1 percent during the first 9 months of 1977 to 65.1 percent during the comparable period in 1979. The airlines increased the number of seats per aircraft by 8.6 percent for the large DC-10s and L-1011s, and by 4.3 percent for the smaller 727s. Finally, airlines have used their aircraft fleets more intensively. Airborne hours per aircraft per day rose by 12 percent between the third quarter of 1977 and the third quarter of 1979. Greater use of the airlines' capital stock has reduced passenger comfort and curtailed some other amenities, but the lower fares it permits compensates for these reductions in service.

The record under regulation offers an instructive contrast. During the mid-1970s, airline input prices also rose substantially; in 1977 they averaged 56 percent above their level of 1973. During this period, however, the airlines lacked the strong spur to productivity brought about by deregulation. Fares rose by 32 percent. Although airlines' profits have weakened during recent months, orders for new, fuel-efficient aircraft have continued to be strong. The difficulty of obtaining long-term credit, which accompanied some industry downturns in the past, as yet shows little sign of occurring.

The experience of the airlines during this past year differs sharply from that of certain segments of the regulated trucking industry. Here lack of fuel, large fuel price increases, and sticky Interstate Commerce Commission rates were significant factors in leading many of the smaller, independent truckers to go on strike rather than operate their trucks at a loss. The result was a shortage of trucking capacity and a disruption in commerce.

It is both impractical and inequitable to dismantle regulatory institutions overnight. Producers and consumers, as well as suppliers and others indirectly dependent on the industry, must have time to adjust to a less regulated market environment, and some may be hurt by less stringent regulation. Transitions must therefore be planned for the groups seriously affected by the change. For this reason the Airline Deregulation Act of 1978 permits a gradual phase-out of the Civil Aeronautics Board's regulatory activity and of the Board itself over a 6-year period. The act also provides continued subsidies for essential service to communities affected by the easing of abandonment restrictions.

Substantially relaxing detailed economic regulation of an industry does not mean the end of governmental interest in the industry's performance. For example, the eventual abolition of the Civil Aeronautics Board will not weaken the powers of the Federal Aviation Administration to regulate airline safety. The Administration is committed to basic reforms in economic regulation and to incorporating in them the adjustments needed to ease the legitimate problems of transition. The President has introduced or is supporting legislation embodying these principles, which would substantially reduce Federal regulation in trucking, railroads, telecommunications, and finance. As the record of airline deregulation has so graphically illustrated, these initiatives offer the prospect of large gains in productivity.

The Carter Administration's trucking bill proposed a sharp reduction in regulatory barriers to competition. Among other things, the bill will make entry into common-carrier trucking easier and will phase out the numerous commodity and route restrictions which limit competition between firms in this segment of the industry. It will significantly broaden the exemption from regulation currently enjoyed by the transporters of some agricultural commodities and permit the Commission to grant similar exemptions to other classes of commodities, if this seems in the public interest. The bill permits freight forwarders and contract carriers to hold common-carrier certificates and ends the artificial limit on the number of shippers that contract carriers may serve. Private carriers will be allowed to apply for authority to haul noncompany commodities, to provide transportation for corporate subsidiaries, and to "trip-lease" for single trips to carriers holding certificates. Finally, it will end the exemption granted in 1948 (over President Truman's veto) of rate bureaus' activities from antitrust litigation. Because of the Administration's belief that truck safety is currently inadequate, the Administration's bill would substantially increase the government's responsibility for this activity and the Federal resources channeled into it.

The Administration's efforts are also directed at broadening the gains achieved by earlier reform legislation affecting railroads. The intent of this legislation has been blunted by the Interstate Commerce Commission's overly restrictive interpretation of certain of its key provisions. The Administration is working with the Congress to see how increased pricing flexibility can be achieved in ways that do not reduce the protection offered "captive" shippers, and it has also sought to make abandonment of unprofitable services less difficult.

In his September 1979 message on telecommunications policy President Carter supported congressional efforts to amend the Communications Act of 1934. Consumers are already benefiting from Federal Communications Commission (FCC) actions that have increased competition in the market for telephone sets and for certain sophisticated data-processing and private-line services. But in spite of extraordinary technological advances that now make it possible to hold meetings, transmit messages, perform research, bank, shop, and receive a widening variety of information and entertainment through electronics—and that invalidate the assumption that all telecommunications enterprises are natural monopolies—the basic statutory framework for regulating telecommunications has remained unchanged. The President's message encouraged legislation to promote competition wherever it is workable. (If necessary, some markets, such as local telephone exchanges, may remain regulated monopolies indefinitely.) He also urged removal of restrictions based on out-of-date market distinctions, such as that between telecommunications and data processing, and he advocated allowing the FCC to develop more efficient means of assigning nonbroadcast frequencies. At the same time, the President reaffirmed the Administration's support for regulations to make basic telephone service available to all at affordable rates and for measures to protect the technical quality of the telecommunications network.

In May 1979 the President sent a financial reform message to the Congress urging that deposit interest rates be permitted to rise to market levels after a period of orderly transition, and that federally insured institutions be authorized to offer interest-bearing transactions accounts to individuals. The President also urged the Congress to grant all federally chartered savings institutions the power to offer variable rate mortgages and to invest up to 10 percent of their assets in consumer loans. This package was intended to bring the benefits of market rates to small savers, promote a steadier flow of credit to finance housing, and improve the efficiency of financial markets. Although a bill was passed by the Senate which addressed all of the President's May proposals, the House-passed bill was less comprehensive. Resolution of the broader questions was postponed until 1980, but the Congress did pass more limited legislation extending through March 31, 1980, authority for credit union share drafts, automatic transfer services, and savings and loan institutions' remote service units. These three services effectively enable depositors to earn interest on deposits that are used for making current transactions.

BALANCING COSTS AND BENEFITS IN INDIVIDUAL REGULATIONS

Eliminating large areas of regulation is not the appropriate route to reform of regulations aimed at environmental protection, health, safety, and other social goals. Rather, attention must focus on the processes and techniques of regulation. One especially important task is to ensure that the individual regulations consider the balance between gains and social costs and the adoption of cost-effective approaches.

The designing of any regulation involves an implicit weighing of costs against benefits. How explicit any such balancing should be or can be is a major question, especially in regulation affecting the environment, health, and safety. Although any explicit effort to determine the "appropriate" level of health and safety meets with opposition, many similar choices are being made implicitly. It is clear, for example, that traffic fatalities could be reduced by drastically lowering maximum speed limits or by providing pedestrian underpasses at all major traffic intersections. The failure of society to take these actions reflects a tacit judgment that the benefits in safety do not warrant the costs. Society also implicitly recognizes that a risk-free world is impossible, and that pursuing such a goal would lead to unacceptable reductions in social welfare. Indeed, reducing some risks can generate new risks elsewhere. For example, prohibiting the use of sodium nitrite as a meat preservative may cut the risk of cancer but increase the risk of botulism.

The Administration sought to encourage balanced and cost-effective regulation through the requirement for regulatory analysis called for in Executive Order 12044, signed by the President on March 23, 1978, which applies to executive branch agencies and departments but not to the independent regulatory agencies. The order requires that agencies' policy makers give increased attention to regulatory issues, provide greater opportunity for public participation in the development of regulation, and conduct "sunset" reviews of existing regulations. In addition, the order requires that agencies prepare a regulatory analysis for each major regulation. The analysis must examine the costs and other burdens imposed by the proposed regulatory action and compare them with those of alternative actions differing in approach, timing, degree of stringency, or scope.

The purpose of regulatory analysis is not to reduce all costs and benefits to dollar sums that can be mechanically compared. Some monetary costs cannot be confidently estimated—the costs, for example, of introducing untested changes in technology or production processes, or of changing the attributes of products or the location of plants. Even more clearly, many social benefits cannot be easily converted to monetary terms. But costs and burdens can be identified and in many cases measured. Benefits can be described and often analyzed at least partially in quantitative terms even if not in dollars.

The fundamental premise of the requirement for regulatory analysis is that the difficulty of measuring costs and benefits justifies neither indiscriminate regulation nor the elimination of all regulation. The analysis required by the Executive Order is not a cost-benefit analysis which automatically dictates the decision; it is a procedural mechanism—a decision-making tool—for examining the costs and other consequences of achieving regulatory goals.

Regulatory analyses are not easy to prepare, but they play an important role. A formal regulatory analysis forces the rulemaking agency to consider explicitly the objectives of a major regulation and the best route to those goals. It requires consideration of process as well as outcome. This sort of thinking is a prerequisite for good rulemaking.

A draft regulatory analysis is issued when a regulation is first proposed. It can thus play a part in the public debate over the rule. Members of the public can examine and evaluate the agency's assumptions and objectives. The President has also established an interagency group to review and comment upon selected regulatory analyses. The Regulatory Analysis Review Group comprises representatives from the Executive Office of the President and from all executive branch economic and regulatory agencies. This group, which is chaired by the Council of Economic Advisers, has completed five comprehensive reviews during each of the past 2 years. In 1979 this group's reports, submitted for the public record, covered the Environmental Protection Agency's hazardous waste standards and new source performance standards for electric utility plants; the Department of Energy's proposed and interim final regulations on coal conversion for utilities and industrial boilers; and the Department of Health, Education, and Welfare's proposal for labeling to accompany prescription drugs. At year's end, reports were being prepared reviewing the Environmental Protection Agency's air carcinogen policy, its guidelines for water effluents in the leather-tanning industry, and the Department of Energy's standards for the energy performance of new buildings.

The Carter Administration proposed a permanent requirement for regulatory analysis. Agency heads would be required either to choose the least burdensome alternative or to explain their proposed course of action. Selecting the least burdensome alternative would not be mandatory if there were a justification for choosing another approach. The relevant substantive statute would continue to govern the final decision.

Several existing statutes have been interpreted as limiting the extent to which regulatory agencies can consider costs (including added risks). However, even for agencies having little or no discretion to balance costs against benefits, the regulatory analysis allows consideration of cost effectiveness. If even this degree of flexibility is not within the terms of the statute, the rationale for precluding cost effectiveness should be continuously re-evaluated in the light of new knowledge. The Administration supported "sunset" review legislation that would require just such periodic re-examination of major regulatory mandates.

COORDINATING REGULATORY PROGRAMS

Improving individual regulations is an important part of long-term economic policy, but more is needed for effective management of the regulatory process. Many individual regulations overlap, and some try to serve conflicting objectives. For example, congressionally mandated emission standards for automobiles have sometimes tended to decrease fuel economy. When they do this, they make it harder for auto companies to meet the Department of Transportation's standards requiring a steady increase in fuel economy. This is not a case of confused action but of conflicting goals. In designing an automobile, some balancing may be necessary between cleaner air and energy conservation.

President Carter established a Regulatory Council, composed of 36 Federal departments and agencies, to help achieve better coordination among regulatory programs and expand efforts to manage the regulatory process more effectively. At the President's direction the Council prepares the semiannual *Calendar of Federal Regulations.* This provides in one document a concise summary and analysis of important regulations being developed by each of the executive branch agencies and by those independent regulatory agencies that choose to participate. It includes all major rulemakings in progress or expected during the coming year and thus provides a means of identifying potential overlaps or conflicts as well as previewing the impact of the rules on affected sectors.

The Regulatory Council assessed the cumulative effects of regulations issued by a number of different agencies on particular sectors or industries. The Council began a comprehensive analysis of how regulation affects the automobile industry, and it conducted projects related to coal, hospitals, and nonferrous metals. In addition, the Council successfully coordinated a joint policy statement by the five Federal agencies with primary responsibility for regulating carcinogens. The activities of the Council should help reduce two of the major sources of unnecessary costs of regulation—uncertainty about regulatory policies and conflict or duplication in regulatory actions.

SETTING PRIORITIES

Because we do not live in a world of unlimited resources we cannot simultaneously achieve all desirable social goals. Rational social regulation requires priorities in our use of the resources at hand. No purely technical means can determine what resources should be devoted to social goals in any given year. That must come from the political system. Although some implicit balancing of goals occurs, more explicit attention should be devoted to the aggregate and sectoral consequences of regulation and to the problem of priorities.

Until recently efforts by the Federal Government to promote social goals relied principally on direct expenditures. Since 1921 the Congress has required that these expenditures appear in the Federal budget. The budget process allows explicit tradeoffs to be made and the appropriate level of government action to be debated. But as more goals are pursued through rules and regulations mandating private outlays rather than through direct governmental expenditures, the Federal budget is an increasingly inadequate measure of the resources directed by government toward social ends.

As a result, proposals have been made that the Federal Government develop a "regulatory budget," similar to the expenditure budget, as a framework for looking at the total financial burden imposed by regulations, for setting some limits to this burden, and for making tradeoffs within those limits.

However, a regulatory budget is not without problems. In the case of particular programs in the expenditure budget, past outlays are known and most future outlays can be predicted with some accuracy. Estimates of the past or future costs of regulation, some of which may be important to the development of a regulatory budget, are much less certain. It is difficult, for example, to specify all the costs to a firm when it must locate a new plant according to its third choice rather than its first. It is equally hard to measure the cost of banning the manufacture of a product.

A regulatory budget would also have to take into account the basic difference between the processes through which regulation and expenditures are determined. For Federal expenditures, the President initially sets priorities in the budget he submits to the Congress, which has the final word in adjusting those priorities through appropriation and revenue bills. For social regulations the order is generally reversed. The Congress passes regulatory statutes which set forth objectives with varying specificity. A number of executive branch agencies and independent regulatory agencies are delegated the power, subject to judicial review, to implement those objectives through specific regulations on a case-by-case basis. Regardless of which branch initiates and which completes the priority-setting, however, it is clear that the regulatory process as yet lacks any mechanism analogous to the expenditure budget for comparing and integrating priorities among different program areas.

As the process of regulation develops, more consideration will need to be given to the impact of regulations on the economy. The Nation must recognize that regulation to meet social goals competes for scarce resources with other national objectives. Priorities must be set to make certain that the first problems addressed are those in which regulations are likely to bring the greatest social benefits. Admittedly, this is an ideal that can never be perfectly realized, but tools like the regulatory budget may have to be developed if it is to be approached.

NEW APPROACHES TO REGULATION

Growing recognition that social regulations have significant and sometimes unintended indirect effects on the economy is producing pressure to modify regulatory mechanisms. One modification may take the form of alternatives to, or variations of, the "command-and-control" approach, which uses detailed regulations to specify permissible behavior. This approach often creates inflexibilities that add unnecessarily to the burdens imposed by the regulations. In the past few years regulatory agencies have begun to experiment with alternatives or supplements to traditional regulation. For example, the Environmental Protection Agency has developed an "offset" policy under which firms can set up activities that result in pollution in areas not currently attaining air quality standards only if they can purchase greater reductions in the pollution from existing sources. The agency has also recently promulgated a "bubble" policy, to be applied under carefully controlled conditions, which permits a firm to trade further reductions in emissions from one source for increases in emissions from another. Since firms can thereby reduce pollution most where costs are least, the same overall reduction of pollution can be achieved at a lower cost (or more improvements realized for the same cost). A similar approach was taken in permitting corporate-fleet averaging in the present standards for automobile fuel economy.

Regulation can be improved in other ways as well. Although there is some doubt about the ability of consumers to assess and assimilate certain information, the strategy of informing the public instead of banning questionable products shows promise in some situations. During 1979 the National Highway Traffic Safety Administration made data available to potential buyers on how well cars can withstand crashes, and the Consumer Product Safety Commission continued to publish information about hazardous products as an alternative to outright bans or restrictions. Such programs help consumers become better able to judge competing products.

Increasing the information consumers can draw upon sometimes complements more traditional structural remedies as a means of fostering competition in a market. The Department of Agriculture is currently trying to replicate in the United States the results of a recent Canadian experiment that achieved price reductions of 3 to 7 percent on a typical market basket of food items by disseminating comparative price lists for local grocery stores. If successful, this strategy of fighting high prices by helping consumers take advantage of price differentials among retailers could have wide application.

EFFORTS AT "SMARTER" REGULATION

With the direct encouragement of the President and the Regulatory Council, regulatory agencies have been experimenting with different ways to reduce the cost burden of regulation.

A good example is EPA's "bubble concept." This concept is based on the fact that it is often possible to reduce emissions of a given pollutant from one source far less expensively than from another source. Thus, instead of compelling each source to meet a standard, EPA figuratively places a "bubble" over an area (a large industrial plant, or, in some cases, an even larger geographic area) and lets private decisionmakers decide how to meet the standard for the area at the lowest cost. EPA initially intended to apply the concept quite narrowly, but during 1980 it gradually found ways to broaden its application. Means were found to eliminate many time-consuming procedures. The ability to develop acceptable "bubbles" for sulfur oxides and particulates was demonstrated. Finally, and perhaps most importantly, a solution to a problem once thought to be insurmountable—namely, how to permit the concept to be applied in areas of the country not already meeting ambient air quality standards—appeared to be in sight. As the year came to an end, numerous "bubbles" were in the final stages of design and approval.

In some situations where the bubble concept is applied the cost savings will approach 60 percent. Furthermore, the concept so increases engineering flexibility that it offers the prospect of sharply reduced emissions in some cases.

Experimentation with a second regulatory innovation—the use of marketable permits—is just beginning. EPA recently suggested an overall limit on fluorocarbon production (and, hence, fluorocarbon emissions), combined with the creation of a market for buying and selling emission rights. While this approach promises substantial savings in the cost of reducing emissions, it transfers income from fluorocarbon users and producers to the government. If ways can be found to deal with the income transfer issues, and certain other technical difficulties overcome, the use of such a strategy would permit the continued use of fluorocarbons in those products that consumers value most while eliminating the need for administrative agency determinations of "essential" and "nonessential" uses. It will also stimulate the development of products that make more efficient use of these chemicals.

A third kind of effort at "smarter" regulation is the attempt to tailor regulations to the organization being regulated. The burden of compliance (especially the paperwork burden) often falls disproportionately on small businesses, some local governments, and certain nonprofit organizations. While a blanket exemption of small entities from regulation would not be feasible, it is often possible to reduce their regulatory burden. This approach was incorporated into statute by the Regulatory Flexibility Act of 1980, which requires the Federal Government to estimate the costs of new regulations for small organizations and to review its existing regulations to see whether the burden could be reduced.

Another way of improving the regulatory process is to examine existing regulations in a systematic way and eliminate those that are outmoded or unnecessary. On the basis of such a review, the Occupational Safety and Health Administration (OSHA) has eliminated nearly one thousand regulations during the past 4 years. And in September the Department of Housing and Urban Development (HUD) proposed to eliminate significant portions of its Minimum Property Standards, a large body of regulations going back almost 40 years. These regulations had been originally designed to ensure, among other things, that federally assisted housing is safe and sanitary, and that federally guaranteed mortgages are marketable. HUD's review of the entire set of regulations was prompted by its belief that the private market now adequately performs some of these functions.

Still other alternatives to "command-and-control" regulation are possible. In choosing among alternatives, policymakers should seek the least intrusive ways of achieving regulatory goals. As a matter of course, regulators should look for techniques closely matched to the marketplace failure which was the original justification for regulatory intervention. Resort to a command-and-control solution should be the last step considered, not the first or second.

CONCLUSION

Regulation has joined taxation, and the provision of defense and social services as one of the principal activities of government; it has just as much need for effective management. Careful and responsible management of the government's regulatory efforts is all the more vital because many of their effects on the economy are subtle and difficult to discern. Although some regulation can be largely or wholly eliminated, most of the government's regulatory activities are here to stay. This country will not give up the protection afforded by these programs, any more than it will give up education or a sound defense. But it has every right to demand its dollar's worth. The Administration's regulatory reform effort over the past 3 years has been designed to assure just that.

READING 14

Pollution Problems: Must We Foul Our Own Nests?

The high-pitched whistle of departing jets was deafening as John Q. Smith stepped outside the terminal building and walked toward the parking lot. He located his three-year-old car, got it started, paid the parking fee, and wheeled out onto the congested freeway, adding his own small carbon monoxide and hydrocarbon contributions to the pall that hung over the city. On his left the Contaminated Steel Company was belching noxious streams of dense smoke into the heavy air, ably assisted by the nearby coal-burning power and light plant. Where the freeway joined the river's edge, a pulp and paper mill could be seen spewing its wastes into the river. He held his breath as long as he could along the two-mile stretch of road adjoining the stockyards. Then with a sigh of relief he swerved off the freeway and turned down the country road that would take him home. Once out of sight of human habitat, he stopped the car and relieved himself at the side of the road, noting as he did so the accumulating litter of beer cans, paper, and cellophane bags on the shoulder of the road and in the ditch.

John Q.'s house was located on a lake. Since a group of industrial plants had been built along the lakeshore several miles away, it was not as pleasant to swim and water-ski in the lake as it had been previously. The fishing didn't seem to be as good either. Recently he had been having problems with a backed-up sewer, and he wondered as he turned in the driveway if the plumber had been

169

there to clean out the sewer line that reached from the house to the
lake. John Q. had grown up in the great outdoors (this is why he
had built the house on the lake), and he was much concerned about
its deterioration.

Most of us, like John Q. Smith, are concerned about environmental
problems, but we are not quite sure what we can do about them. As
individuals, we seem to believe that we can do little. In fact, we are
likely to add to the problems by thinking that our own bit of pollution is
just a drop in the bucket.

Public reaction to pollution varies a great deal. At one extreme are
the amateur environmentalists, or nature-lovers, who object to everything that decreases the purity of the air and water or that mars the
natural beauty of the landscape. At the other extreme are those who
seem not to value at all clean air, water, and natural beauty. Most of us
are scattered along the line between these two extremes.

A sensible attack on pollution problems requires the use of economic analysis along with inputs from other disciplines—especially the
natural sciences. In particular, economic analysis may help us (1) determine why and under what circumstances economic units pollute; (2)
determine the extent to which pollution control should be exercised;
and (3) evaluate alternative antipollution activities of the government.

WHAT IS POLLUTION?

We will not make much progress in an economic analysis of pollution until we are familiar with both the nature of the environment in
which we live and what it is that constitutes pollution of that environment. We shall consider these two concepts in turn.

The environment and its services

The environment is easily defined. It consists of the air, water, and
land around us. These provide us with a variety of important services.

First, the environment provides a *habitat* or surroundings in which
both plant and animal life can survive. Temperature ranges on the
planet are neither too hot nor too cold for survival. The air, the water,
and the land contain the elements needed to sustain living matter as we
know it.

Second, the environment contains *resources* that are usable in the
production of goods and services. These include minerals such as
petroleum, coal, and a wide assortment of ores that can be processed
into metals and metal alloys. They include soil properties and plant life

supported by the soil. Resources include the plant and animal life yielded by water as well as the inherent properties of water used directly in production processes. They also include oxygen and nitrogen, along with other elements and properties found in the atmosphere.

Third, the environment furnishes many *amenities* that make life more enjoyable. It opens up possibilities of a walk along a river, through an alfalfa field, or in a rose garden. It provides an area in which you can fly kites or have picnics, a place to take your girlfriend or your boyfriend—or even your husband or your wife. You can sit in it and enjoy the sunset. Or, if you so desire, you can paint it or photograph it.

The services of the environment are used by production units and household units as they engage in activities of various kinds. Production units lay heavy claims on the environment's resources, but they may also make use of its habitat and amenity characteristics.

As production units engage in the process of transforming raw and semifinished materials into goods and services that will satisfy human wants, there are at least three ways in which the environment can be affected. First, some of the environment's stocks of exhaustible resources may be diminished. These include coal, petroleum, and many mineral deposits. Second, it is called upon for replaceable resources like timber, grassland, oxygen, and nitrogen. Third, it is used as a place to dispose of the wastes of the production and consumption processes—as a gigantic garbage disposal.

Recycling of wastes and the concept of pollution

The pollution problem arises primarily from the use of the environment by producers and consumers as a dumping ground for wastes. We litter the countryside with cans, paper, and the other residues of consumption and production. We dump the emissions from our automobiles and factories into the atmosphere. We empty sewage and residue from production directly and indirectly into streams, rivers, and lakes.

As wastes from production and consumption are dumped into the environment, nature sets recycling processes in motion. Animals use oxygen, giving off carbon dioxide wastes. But plants use carbon dioxide, giving off oxygen wastes. Dead plants and animal life are attacked by chemical elements that decompose them, restoring to the soil elements that the living organisms had withdrawn from it. Living organisms frequently contribute to the decomposition process. Iron and steel objects rust and disintegrate over time. So does wood and other matter. Wastes that can be decomposed in air, water, and soil are said to be *biodegradable*. But there are some wastes that are not biodegradable. Aluminum containers like beer cans are a case in point.

Recycling—the transformation of wastes into raw materials that are again usable—requires variable lengths of time, depending on what it is that is being recycled. It takes many years for a steel pipe to rust away. Wood varies a great deal in the time it takes for its complete disintegration. But many plant and animal products require only a very short time to decompose.

Pollution consists of loading the environment with wastes that are not completely recycled, are not recycled fast enough, or are not recycled at all. It involves a diminution of the capacity of the environment to yield environmental services. Pollution occurs when recycling processes fail to prevent wastes from accumulating in the environment.

Common forms of pollution

Pollution is as old as civilization itself. Wherever people have congregated, their wastes have tended to pile up more rapidly than the forces of nature can digest them. As long as the world was sparsely populated and no permanent cities existed, no great problems were created. When the extent of pollution in one locale imposed costs on the people living there that outweighed the costs associated with moving, they simply moved away from it. Then, given time, natural recycling processes could in many cases take over and restore the excess wastes to usable form.

When towns and cities came into existence, pollution raised more serious problems. How could body wastes from humans and animals, as well as refuse from the daily round of living, be disposed of? Until fairly recent times it was not disposed of in many instances—levels of sanitation were unbelievably low, and levels of stench were unbelievably high. As the density of the world's population has increased and as it has become more difficult to move away from pollution problems, the human race has turned its attention more and more toward the development of control measures. But in order to control pollution, it must be identified as accurately as possible in its various forms.

Air pollution. In the processes of production and consumption, five major kinds of wastes are dumped into the atmosphere. Most are a result of combustion and have caused local problems for a long time. Since there are millions of cubic miles of atmosphere to absorb these wastes, however, air pollution has not caused great concern until the past few decades. These wastes are carbon monoxide, sulfur oxides, nitrogen oxides, hydrocarbons, and particulates.

Carbon monoxide, an odorless, colorless gas, makes the atmosphere a less hospitable habitat for animal life. In concentrated amounts, it causes dizziness, headaches, and nausea in humans. Exposure to a sufficiently high concentration—about 100 parts per 1 million parts of atmosphere—for a few hours can be fatal. About 64 percent of the carbon monoxide emissions into the atmosphere in the United States comes from automobiles, and another 12 percent comes from industrial sources of one kind or another.[1] The greatest concentrations of carbon monoxide occur in large cities. On New York City streets concentration levels as high as 13 parts per 1 million parts of atmosphere have been recorded.

Sulfur oxides constitute a second major source of atmospheric pollution. Where they are heavily concentrated, they cause damage to both plant and animal life. Oxides result largely from the combustion of fuel oils and coal. Consequently, high levels of concentration are most likely to occur where these are used for the generation of electricity and for residential heating.

A third atmospheric pollutant is *nitrogen oxides*. These can cause lung damage in human beings and may also retard plant growth. The main sources of the pollutant are automobiles and stationary combustion processes such as those used in generating electric power.

Hydrocarbons constitute a fourth kind of waste emitted into the air. At their present concentration levels no direct harmful effects have been attributed to them. However, they combine with nitrogen oxides and ultraviolet rays of the sun to form photochemical smog. The smog may produce breathing difficulties and eye irritation for human beings. In addition, it speeds up the oxidation processes to which paints and metals are subject, resulting in substantial damages to industrial plants and equipment. More than 50 percent of hydrocarbon emissions in the United States comes from automobiles, and the rest from other combustion processes.

A fifth air pollutant consists of a heterogeneous mixture of suspended solids and liquids called *particulates*. These are largely dust and ash, along with lead from automobile exhausts. The major source of particulates, however, is fuel combustion in stationary sources and in industrial processes. Open fires used to burn trash and garbage also make their contributions. Particulates lower visibilities. Some, such as lead from automobile exhausts, may be directly harmful to human beings.

Water pollution. Water pollution is ordinarily measured in terms of the capacity of water to support aquatic life. This capacity depends upon (1) the level of dissolved oxygen in the water and (2) the presence of matters or materials injurious to plant and animal life.

---

[1] U.S. Department of Health, Education, and Welfare, National Air Pollution Control Administration, *Nationwide Inventory of Air Pollutant Emissions, 1968,* August 1971.

The level of dissolved oxygen is built up through aeration of water and through the photosynthetic processes of plant life living in the water. It is destroyed by its use to decompose organic matter that occurs in or is dumped into the water. The oxygen needed for decomposition purposes is referred to as *biochemical oxygen demand,* or BOD. The level of dissolved oxygen available for supporting aquatic life, then, depends upon the balance between aeration and photosynthesis on the one hand and BOD on the other.

The level of dissolved oxygen is affected by several factors. First, it tends to be higher the greater the amount of a given volume of water exposed to the atmosphere. In nature, fast-running streams, rapids, and waterfalls contribute to aeration. Artificial aeration is frequently accomplished by shooting streams of water through the air. Second, it tends to be higher the greater the amount of photosynthesis that occurs in the water. In some instances the amount of photosynthesis that occurs in aquatic plant life may be reduced by air pollution. In this way, air pollution may be a source of water pollution. Third, it tends to be higher the lower the temperature of the water—use of the water for cooling by firms such as steel mills, oil refineries, and electricity-generating plants raises the temperature of the water and lowers its capacity to hold dissolved oxygen. Fourth, organic wastes that create BOD come from both domestic and industrial sources, so the level of dissolved oxygen varies inversely with the amounts that are dumped. The decomposition of such wastes can be greatly facilitated and BOD can be correspondingly reduced by chemical treatment of such wastes before they are discharged into streams, rivers, lakes, or oceans.

The capacity of water to support aquatic life is reduced when various kinds of materials and matters are dumped into it. Among these are toxins which do not settle out of the water and are not easily broken down by biological means. Mercury is a toxin that has created problems of contamination in tuna and salmon. So are phenols, herbicides, and pesticides. There have been heated discussions in recent years over the propriety of using them in large quantities. Questions have been raised also as to whether the oceans should be used for the dumping of nuclear wastes and for undersea nuclear explosions.

Land pollution.   Land pollution results from the dumping of a wide variety of wastes on the terrain and from tearing up the earth's surface through such activities as strip mining. Highways are littered with refuse thrown from passing automobiles. Junkyards grow as we scrap over 7 million automobiles per year, to say nothing of the prodigious amounts of other machinery and appliances that are retired from use. Garbage dumps and landfills grow as towns and cities dispose of the solid wastes they collect and accumulate. All of these reduce the capacity of the terrain to render environmental services.

The growing emphasis on coal as an energy source creates mounting concern over the effects of mining on the landscape. Strip mining has typically left unsightly blemishes on the countryside. Can and should the mined area be restored? In pit mining areas can and should steps be taken to make slag and rock piles more attractive esthetically?

ECONOMICS OF POLLUTION

No one likes pollution. Almost everyone would like to see something done about it. Toward this end we consider in this section the fundamental economics of the pollution problem. We shall examine the reasons pollution occurs, analyze the effects of pollution on resource allocation, look at the costs of pollution control, and identify its benefits. We shall attempt to establish criteria for determining the appropriate level of control.

Why polluters pollute

Why is it that pollution occurs? What is there about environmental services that causes consumers and producers to use the environment as a free dumping ground? Ordinarily, pollution results from one or both of two basic factors: (1) the fact that no one has property rights or enforces them in the environment being polluted, and (2) the collectively consumed characteristics of the environment being polluted.

If no one owns a portion of the environment or if an owner cannot police it or have it policed, then it becomes possible for people to use a river, a lake, the air, or an area of land as a wastebasket without being charged for doing so. Because no one owns the air above city streets and highways, automobile owners can dump combustion gases into it without paying for the privilege of doing so. Similarly, a paper mill can dump its wastes into the river without charge because no one owns the river. But even ownership of the environment may not be enough to keep pollution from occurring. How many times have you seen litter accumulate on a vacant lot, or junk dumped in a ditch in a pasture away from town, because the owner was not there to prevent the dumping?

In addition, many environmental services are collectively consumed or used. It is hard to single out and determine the value of the air that one person—or an automobile—uses. Similarly, it is often difficult to attach a value to the water deterioration caused by one industrial plant when thousands dump their wastes into a river. Would any one person be willing to pay someone *not* to take an action that would destroy a beautiful view across the countryside? When values cannot be placed on the amounts of environmental services used by any one person, it is difficult to induce people not to pollute by charging them for the right to do so.

Pollution and resource use

In the process of polluting the environment, polluters impose spill-over costs on others. Polluters' costs are thus reduced below what they would be in the absence of pollution. Similarly, costs to others (nonpolluters) of using environmental services are greater than they would be if there were no pollution. Polluters, then, are induced to overuse environmental services at the expense of other users, and other users of the polluted environment are induced to underuse them. Thus, pollution involves inefficient use or misallocation of environmental services among those who use them.

Suppose, for example, that two industries are located along a riverbank. An industry producing paper is located upstream, using the river as a place to discharge its wastes. Downstream is a power-generating industry that requires large amounts of clean water for cooling purposes. If the paper industry were not there, the water from the river would be clean enough for the power industry to use. But since it is there—just upstream—the firms in the power industry must clean the water before using it.

Since the use of the river by one set of parties as a dumping place for wastes may reduce the value of the river's services to other users, a transfer of costs may be incurred by the dumping. If recycling of the dumped wastes occurs fast enough, or if the environment is large enough relative to the wastes dumped into it so that no one is injured by the dumping, no cost or pollution problems occur.

The use of the river for waste disposal by the paper industry decreases the value of the river's services for power production in the example, so cost transfers are involved in that dumping. In effect, the paper industry shifts some of its costs of production to the power industry. It is the power industry that must pay for cleaning the water, but it is the paper industry that makes it dirty.

Consider first the power industry situation if there were no pollution by the paper industry. In Figure 14–1, the demand curve for power is D_eD_e and the supply curve in the absence of pollution is S_eS_e. The equilibrium output is e and the equilibrium price is p_e per kilowatt-hour. The cost of producing a kilowatt-hour at output level e is also p_e.

FIGURE 14–1

Effects of water pollution on water users

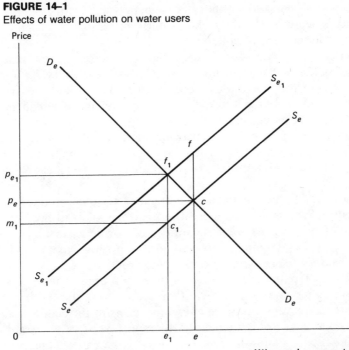

The demand curve for the output of the power industry is D_eD_e. Its supply curve, when it can obtain clean water for its use, is S_eS_e. Consequently, it will produce and sell e kilowatt-hours per day. However, if a paper industry located upstream pollutes the water, costs of cleaning the water before using it move the supply curve upward (or to the left). The power industry accordingly reduces its output to e_1 and raises its price to p_{e1}. The power industry—or its customers—thus pays the costs of cleaning the paper industry's wastes from the water.

Suppose, now, that the power industry must clean the water before using it. Since it must cover its costs, the price that it must receive in order to induce it to produce any specific quantity of electricity will be higher by an amount equal to the costs per kilowatt-hour of cleaning the water. The supply curve is thus shifted upward by that amount—c_1f_1 or cf—to some position such as $S_{e1}S_{e1}$. If the output of the power industry were e_1 kilowatt-hours, the price necessary to bring forth that output in the absence of pollution is e_1c_1. With pollution occurring, the necessary price is e_1f_1 or p_{e1}, with c_1 being the cost per kilowatt-hour of cleaning the water. Similarly, for an output level of e, the required price in the absence of pollution is ec, with pollution it is *ef,* and the cost per kilowatt-hour of cleaning is *cf.* So the supply of electricity is decreased by the pollution of the paper industry from what it would be in absence of pollution.

The effects of the decrease in the supply of electricity are a smaller quantity bought and sold, a higher price paid by consumers, and a lower return to producers than would be the case without the paper industry's pollution of the water. The quantity exchanged is reduced to e_1; the price paid by consumers goes up to p_{e_1}; and the return to producers after paying the cleaning costs for water decrease from p_e to m_1 per kilowatt-hour. Thus, we see that the costs of pollution by the paper industry are borne by both the consumers and the producers of electricity.

In addition, the power industry is induced to underproduce. The supply curve $S_e S_e$ shows the alternative costs per kilowatt-hour to the economy of producing various quantities of power when unpolluted water is used. For example, at output level *e,* it shows that *ec* dollars must be paid for the resources necessary to produce one kilowatt-hour at this level of output. This is what those resources could earn in alternative employments; it is what they are worth in those other employments, and it represents the alternative costs to the economy of a kilowatt-hour of electricity. Similarly, at output level e_1, the *alternative cost* of producing a kilowatt-hour is $e_1 c_1$. With the paper industry polluting the river, however, consumers pay $e_1 f_1$ per kilowatt-hour, which is more than the costs of production. Wherever consumers are willing to pay more for an item than it costs to produce it, it is usually desirable that output be expanded. But this will not happen in the power industry because, in addition to the costs of producing electricity, it must incur an additional outlay, $c_1 f_1$, to clean the water; that is, to undo what the paper industry has done.

The supply curve of the paper industry is increased by its access to the river for waste disposal. In Figure 14–2 let $S_r S_r$ be the paper industry's supply curve, assuming that the river is *not* available as a "free" dumping space. The supply curve shows the alternative prices that must be received by the paper industry to induce it to produce and sell various quantities of paper. To induce it to produce and sell *r* reams, the price per ream must be *rg.* To induce it to place r_1 reams on the market, the price must be $r_1 g_1$. Suppose now that the river is made available to the paper industry as a "free" dumping ground for wastes. The costs of producing a ream of paper are now reduced, and for an output level of *r* reams per day the price need not be higher than *rh*—if the cost saving per ream is *hg.* Similarly, for r_1 reams and a cost saving of $h_1 g_1$, the necessary price is $r_1 h_1$. The supply curve of paper is thus

FIGURE 14–2
Effects of water pollution on the polluter

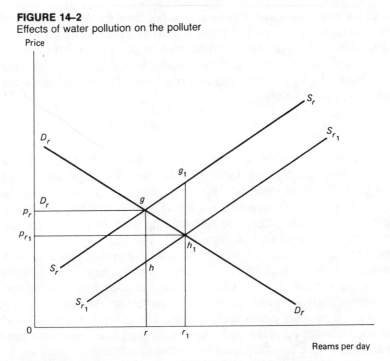

The demand curve for the output of the paper industry is D_rD_r. When it must clean its own wastes, its supply curve is S_rS_r, and its output level will be r reams of paper per day. If it can dump its wastes into the river, cleaning costs are saved, and its supply curve shifts downward (to the right). Its output will increase to r_1. It is able to shift a part of its costs to downstream users of the water.

shifted to the right by the accessibility of the river as a "free" place to dispose of its wastes.

The same type of reasoning that tells us the power industry underproduces because of the paper industry's pollution also tells us the paper industry overproduces. In Figure 14–2, D_rD_r is the demand curve for paper. If the paper industry were to bear the costs of its dumping of wastes by leaving clean water for the power plant, its supply curve would be S_rS_r; its price would be p_r; and its output level would be r. However, since it is able to use the river for waste disposal, its supply curve becomes $S_{r_1}S_{r_1}$, and it produces r_1 reams of paper per day, selling it at a price of p_{r_1} per ream. The evidence of overproduction is that *alternative costs* per ream of paper exceed what consumers pay to get it. The alternative costs per ream are r_1g_1. Of this amount, r_1h_1 is the cost to the paper industry of resources other than waste disposal used in the production of a ream of paper at output level r_1, and h_1g_1 is the cost of waste disposal that is transferred to the power industry per ream of paper produced. This latter amount is not taken into account by the paper industry, so the true cost of a ream of paper exceeds what it is worth to consumers.

The costs of controlling pollution

Our reactions to pollution often take the form of, "Let's wipe it out." We maintain that we are entitled to clean air, clean water, and clean land. But how clean is clean? Cleanliness, like goodness, is a relative rather than an absolute quality. To determine the amount of pollution, if any, that should be allowed, the *costs* of keeping the environment clean must first be considered.

Pollution control is not costless. An industrial plant that scrubs or cleans its combustion gases before discharging them into the air must use resources in the process. Labor and capital go into the making and operation of antipollution devices, and resources so used are not available to produce other goods and services. The value of the goods and services that must be given up is the cost of the plant's pollution control activities. The cost of pollution control is a straightforward application of the alternative-cost principle.

The costs of pollution control to society are illustrated graphically by the production possibilities curve of Figure 14–3. Dollars' worth of all goods and services other than pollution control are measured on the vertical axis, and dollars' worth of pollution control are measured on the horizontal axis. At point A_1 the labor and capital of the economy are producing q_1 dollars' worth of goods and services and c_1 dollars' worth of antipollution activities. If still more pollution control—a cleaner environment—is desired, some value of goods and services must be sacrificed. By giving up q_2q_1 dollars' worth of goods and services, pollution control can be increased by c_1c_2 dollars' worth. Thus, q_2q_1 dollars' worth of goods and services is the economic cost of an additional c_1c_2 dollars' worth of control or of a cleaner environment.

The benefits of controlling pollution

The benefits of pollution control consists of the increase in the well-being of the members of the society that results from pollution control activities. To measure the benefits of a pollution control activity, the value of the increase in well-being that it generates must be

FIGURE 14–3
The costs of pollution control

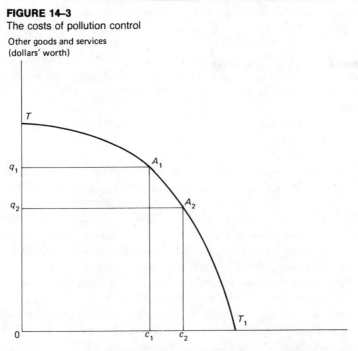

Other goods and services
(dollars' worth)

Pollution control (dollars' worth)

The combinations of other goods and services and pollution control that the resources of the economy can support are shown by the production possibilities curve TT_1. By giving up q_1T dollars' worth of other goods and services, the economy can have c_1 dollars' worth of pollution control, as shown at point A_1. If c_1c_2 more dollars' worth of pollution control are to be obtained, the cost will be q_2q_1 additional dollars' worth of other goods and services.

determined. Suppose, for example, that smog permeates a particular metropolitan area but that pollution control activities can reduce or perhaps even eliminate it. To determine the benefits of, say, a 50 percent reduction in smog, we can ask each individual living in the area how much such a reduction would be worth personally. By totaling all the replies we would arrive at the dollar value of the expected benefits.

The appropriate level of pollution control

Since pollution control—a cleaner environment—has costs, society must make a choice between the level of goods and services its resources will be used to produce and the degree of cleanliness of its

a trade-off exists

environment. If the society experiences a level of pollution that is distasteful to it, it will be willing to sacrifice some quantities of goods and services for some level of pollution control.

The appropriate level of pollution control is determined by weighing its benefits against its costs. If the benefits of additional control—what cleaner air is worth to the citizens of the society—exceed the costs of the additional control, then pollution control should be increased. However, if the benefits of additional control are less than what it costs in terms of sacrificed goods and services, the additional control is unwarranted.

As an illustration, consider a community of 10,000 persons that is pervaded by a nauseating stench from an incinerator used to dispose of the community's garbage. Suppose that the odor can be completely eliminated by an expenditure of $100,000 per year for an alternate method of garbage disposal (carrying it away and burying it in a landfill outside the town) and that it can be partially controlled by using various combinations of burning and burying.

Suppose that the costs of different levels of partial control are those of columns one, two, and three of Table 14–1. By spending $10,000 on carrying and burying, the community can eliminate 10 percent of the stench; each additional $10,000 expenditure eliminates another 10 percent of the original total stench, until with a $100,000 expenditure the pollution is entirely eliminated.

Column three of Table 14–1 lists the *marginal costs* of pollution control. The concept is essentially the same as the marginal costs of crime prevention—it shows the change in total costs per unit change in the amount of pollution control. Since each increment in pollution control

TABLE 14–1
Annual costs and benefits of pollution control

(1)	(2)	(3)	(4)	(5) Community	(6)	(7)
Pollution control or eliminated stench	Total cost of control ($000)	Marginal cost of control ($000)	Per person marginal benefits of control	marginal benefits of control ($000)	Total benefits of control ($000)	Net benefits of control ($000)
1st 10%	$ 10	$10	$10.00 ea.	$100	$100	$ 90
2d 10	20	10	8.00	80	180	160
3d 10	30	10	6.00	60	240	210
4th 10	40	10	4.00	40	280	240
5th 10	50	10	2.00	20	300	250
6th 10	60	10	1.60	16	316	256
7th 10	70	10	1.20	12	328	258
8th 10	80	10	0.80	8	336	256
9th 10	90	10	0.40	4	340	250
10th 10	100	10	0.20	1	341	241

(an increment is defined as 10 percent of the control needed to eliminate the odor) adds $10,000 to the total cost of pollution control, the marginal cost of pollution control at each control level is $10,000.

The benefits of pollution control to the community are shown in columns four, five, and six. Before any control is undertaken, each person in the community is asked for an opinion of what a 10 percent reduction in the stench is worth. Suppose each person indicates a willingness to pay $10 for it. We conclude that $100,000 measures the total benefits yielded by the first 10 percent reduction. Since the benefits exceed the costs by $90,000, the first 10 percent reduction is clearly warranted.

The question now arises as to whether a second 10 percent reduction in the stench is worthwhile. Since the pollution is not as intense as it was with no control, a second 10 percent reduction is of less value than was the first one. Suppose each person values the move from 10 percent control to 20 percent control at $8, so that the community valuation of the extra control—or the marginal benefits of it—is $80,000. Since the marginal costs of the additional control are only $10,000, putting it into effect adds $70,000 to the total net benefits of control and is, therefore, a good investment for the community.

Column five shows the community's *marginal benefit* at different levels of control. Marginal benefits of pollution control, like the marginal benefits of crime prevention, are defined as the *change* in total benefits per unit *change* in whatever it is that yields the benefits. Note that the *total benefits* at any given level of control are obtained by adding up the marginal benefits as the level of control is increased unit by unit up to that level.

Marginal benefits, as shown in Table 14–1, decline as the level of pollution control is increased (the level of the stench is decreased). This is what we would expect to happen in the case at hand. The greater the amount of control, or the lower the level of the stench, the less urgent additional control becomes. This will be the usual situation in controlling pollution.

The level of pollution control yielding the maximum net benefits to the people of the community is that at which the marginal benefits just cease to exceed the marginal costs. The marginal benefits of the first two 10 percent increments in the total amount of control needed to eliminate the stench exceed the marginal costs of making them. Thus, net benefits are increased by increasing control at least to the 20 percent level. The third, fourth, fifth, sixth, and seventh 10 percent increments also yield marginal benefits exceeding their marginal costs, and they increase the net benefits of control to the community. Now consider the eighth 10 percent increment. Marginal benefits are $8,000, and marginal costs are $10,000. Extending pollution control from the 70 percent level to the 80 percent level *reduces* the net benefits by $2,000. The eighth 10 percent increment is not worth to the community what it costs.

The principle is perfectly general. Net benefits will always be increased by increasing control if the marginal benefits of the increase are greater than the marginal costs of making it. Net benefits will decrease from an increase in the control level if the marginal benefits of that increase are less than its marginal costs. The appropriate level of control is the one that approaches as closely as possible the one at which the marginal benefits equal the marginal costs but does not go far enough for marginal costs to exceed marginal benefits.

WHAT CAN BE DONE ABOUT POLLUTION?

Human beings often react to problems with their emotions rather than with the capacity for logic with which they are endowed. Policies recommended to control pollution reflect this human characteristic. Typical recommendations call for direct control of pollution by the state. But this is only one of the possible avenues of reducing pollution problems. Others include indirect control by the state through a system of incentives encouraging potential polluters not to pollute or to limit their pollution, and an examination of the institutions of private property rights and markets to see if they can be modified to provide the desired limitations on polluting activities.

Direct controls

An appealingly simple way to control pollution is to have the government ban polluting activities or agents. If phosphates contaminate water, then ban the use of phosphates in detergents. If DDT pollutes water and land, ban the use of DDT. If the burning of fuel oil and coal increases the sulfur oxide content of the atmosphere, prohibit their use. Require industrial plants to clean the pollutants from whatever it is they discharge into the atmosphere or water. The method is straightforward and, on the face of it, seems eminently fair.

Government agencies, notably the Environmental Protection Agency (EPA) at the federal level, use direct controls to reduce many kinds of polluting activities. They set and attempt to enforce emission standards for such polluters as automobiles, power plants, and steel mills. State regulation of polluters, to the extent that it is accomplished, is in general supervised by the EPA.

The case of the city with the terrible stench shows that complete prohibition of pollutants is not likely to be worth its costs. Pollution control uses resources that could have produced goods and services, and the value of the goods and services forgone is the cost to society of controlling the pollution. If the damage done by an additional unit of pollution is less than the costs of preventing it from occurring, community welfare is greater if it is allowed to occur. Consequently, direct controls usually should aim at a less idealistic goal than a pollution-free environment. They may take the form of controlling the level of pollution by such devices as setting emissions standards or limits for industrial plants, automobiles, and other polluters.

One problem raised by the use of direct controls to limit the amount of pollution is that it presupposes the regulatory body can determine what the economically desirable levels of pollution are. This is not an insurmountable problem. Tolerance limits on the amount of pollution to be allowed can be reasonably well established. Within those limits, overall costs can be weighed continually against benefits to establish an approximation of the desirable levels of pollution.

A second problem is the difficulty facing a regulatory body in achieving an efficient allocation of the permissible pollution among different polluters. For example, it may be more costly for a steel mill to eliminate a unit of sulfur oxide from its emissions than it is for a power plant. In the interests of economic efficiency, it is best to eliminate pollution where it is least costly to do so. Thus the power plant should be required to reduce its sulfur oxide emission before the steel mill is required to do so. This is a difficult kind of decision for a regulatory body to make, since it is responsible to a political body for which economic efficiency is not a primary goal. In addition, it is unrealistic to suppose that the regulatory body has a working knowledge of the nature of costs for every polluter.

A third problem is that of enforcing the standards of emissions once it has been determined what those standards should be. Direct controls fail to provide polluters with an economic incentive not to pollute. In fact, it will pay them to seek ways and means to evade the pollution standards set for them. But we should not overstate the enforcement problem. Almost any prohibition of activities that individuals and business firms want to engage in creates enforcement problems.

Indirect controls

It is possible for the government to control many types of pollution by placing taxes on polluting activities. Where the amounts of polluting discharges can be measured for individual polluters, a tax can be placed directly on each unit of discharge. This will induce the polluter to reduce the amount of pollution that is discharged. In some cases where such measurement is not possible, polluters may be taxed indirectly—for example, automobiles not equipped with pollution control devices can be subjected to a tax on a mileage basis. This would induce their owners either to install pollution control devices or to drive less. At this time, not much use has been made of this method of control.

Figure 14–4 illustrates the use of a tax to control the amounts of pollutants discharged into the environment. Consider an industrial concern that discharges its polluting wastes into a river. Processes for cleaning the wastes so that the pollution they cause is eliminated or diminished are available. *Marginal cleaning costs,* defined as the change in total cleaning costs per one unit change in the firm's discharge of wastes, are shown by *MCC*. For example, if the level of discharge is q_0, then q_0A_0 is the *addition* to the firm's total cost of

FIGURE 14–4

Control of pollution by means of a tax on polluted discharges

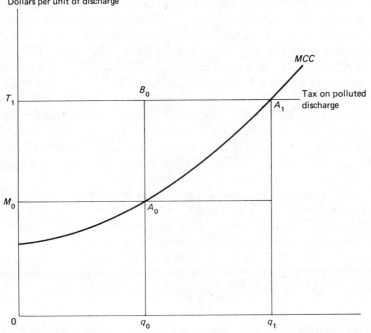

If the level of a tax on polluted discharges exceeds the marginal costs of cleaning the discharge, a firm will elect to clean the discharge. This will be the case for all discharge levels up to q_1. If the level of the tax is less than the marginal cleaning costs, the firm will elect to pay the tax rather than clean the discharge. This will occur for all discharge in excess of q_1.

cleaning brought about when the amount of discharge is increased from one unit less than q_0 to the q_0 level. Similarly, the addition to total cleaning costs when the firm moves from one unit less than q_1 units to q_1 units is $q_1 A_1$. We show the MCC curve sloping upward to the right, indicating that the larger the firm's rate of waste discharge, the greater is the cost to it of cleaning an additional unit. This may or may not be the case—we assume here for illustrative purposes that it is. The level of the tax on polluted discharge is T_1 per unit, regardless of the level of the discharge.

A tax per unit of polluted discharge will induce the firm to reduce its polluting activity if the amount of the tax exceeds the marginal costs of cleaning the discharge. If the discharge is less than q_1, say q_0 units per day, it pays the firm not to pollute. It is less costly to clean the discharge than it is to pay the tax. For the q_0 unit of discharge, $q_0 B_0$ would be added to the firm's total costs if it elects to pay the tax and not to clean up the discharge. Only $q_0 A_0$ would be added to its total costs if it elects to clean the discharge and pay no tax. This will be the case for any discharge level up to q_1 units per day. On the other hand, for a discharge level exceeding q_1 per day, the firm will clean q_1 units and pay the tax on the remainder of the discharge. It is cheaper to clean than to pay the tax on each unit up to that level. For units of discharge exceeding q_1, it is cheaper to pay the tax than to clean them.

The tax can be set at any desired level, depending upon the amount of pollution the government decides to allow. Raising the tax will decrease the amount of pollution, and lowering the tax will increase it. Ideally, the tax should be set at a level at which the marginal benefits to society of cleaning a unit of discharge equal the marginal cleaning costs. If the level of polluted discharge permitted is such that the marginal benefits of cleaning the discharge exceed the marginal costs of cleaning it, the tax is too low and should be increased. If the level of polluted discharge permitted is such that marginal benefits of cleaning are less than the marginal costs of cleaning, the tax is too high and should be decreased.

The use of taxes to control pollution has its advantages. A major one is that it provides an incentive to the polluter to seek improved ways and means of cleaning up its discharge. Another advantage is that it prevents the polluter from shifting some of its production costs (pollution costs) to others; it reduces the incentive to overproduce.

There are also disadvantages. First, it usually is difficult to determine the benefits—total and marginal—to society of cleaning the discharge. Second, enforcement of such a tax is not easy. Policing is necessary to determine that the discharge is indeed properly cleaned. Third, taxes are levied by political rather than economic bodies, and politics may well get in the way of the enactment of appropriate tax levels.

The federal government has used subsidies—the opposite of taxes—extensively as a pollution control measure. These consist primarily of grants made to state and local governments for the construction of sewage treatment facilities. For the fiscal year 1976, almost 54 percent of the estimated federal outlays on pollution control and abatement are for construction of this type.[2] Yet, despite relatively large outlays for water pollution control since passage of the Water Pollution Control Act of 1956, water quality has continued to decrease. Could it be that subsidized treatment of industrial wastes fails to provide incentives to industries to develop or to seek out low-pollution methods of production?

Private property rights

Since the absence of well-defined property rights provides a primary incentive to polluters to dump their wastes in certain segments of the environment, the assignment of property rights either to firms that pollute or to those that benefit from a clean environment may provide a means of control in some cases. Consider, for example, the upstream paper industry—downstream power industry case described earlier. Since neither owns the river, the paper industry is able to use it for waste disposal, and the costs of the waste disposal fall on the power industry.

Suppose that rights to the river are sold at auction by the government. These rights will be purchased by the industry to which they are most valuable. If the annual value to the paper industry of using the river for waste discharges (the costs of alternative means of disposing of the wastes) exceed the annual cost to the power industry of cleaning the water, the paper industry will buy the rights. The river will be put to its most valuable use—that of being a sink for waste disposal. However, if the value of clean water to the power industry (the costs of cleaning it for power industry use) exceeds the value to the paper industry of using the river to discharge wastes, the power industry will purchase the rights and the river will be put to its most productive (valuable) use—that of furnishing clean cooling water for the generation of electricity.

Regardless of which industry buys the rights, changes in the relative

---

[2]Office of Management and Budget, *Special Analysis, Budget of the United States Government, Fiscal Year 1976* (Washington, D.C.: U.S. Government Printing Office, 1975), p. 270.

values of the two uses will provide incentives for the river to be put to the use in which it is most valuable. If the paper industry holds the rights to the river but the annual value of clean water to the power industry exceeds the annual value of the river as a waste disposal, the power industry will be willing to pay the paper industry enough to induce it not to qollute—to use alternative means of disposing of its wastes. On the other hand, if the power industry owns the rights and the annual value of the river to the paper industry as a waste disposal exceeds the annual cost to the power industry of cleaning the water, the power industry will sell the paper industry pollution privileges.

SUMMARY

The environment provides environmental services that are used by both household units and producing units of the economy. In the processes of consumption and production wastes are generated. If the ecological system cannot recycle these wastes as fast as they are generated, wastes accumulate. This constitutes pollution.

Economic analysis of pollution provides a perspective on its causes and its effects, along with the costs and benefits of controlling it. Incentives to pollute stem from (1) an absence of property rights in the environment and (2) the collectively consumed nature of whatever is being polluted. Polluters, by polluting, transfer a part of their costs to others. Cost-benefit analysis is useful in determining how much pollution should be allowed. It indicates that it is seldom in the common interest to forbid pollution altogether.

There are three main avenues that government pollution control policies can take. First, certain polluting activities may be controlled directly through prohibitions or limitations on polluting activities. Second, they may be controlled indirectly by providing polluters with incentives not to qollute—say through taxation of polluting activities. Third, much pollution can be controlled by selling or assigning individuals property rights to whatever is being polluted, then allowing them to sell pollution rights to would-be polluters.